WSH PERLSCRIPT

AND

WBEMSCRIPTING

ASYNC

Working with GetAsync

Richard Thomas Edwards

CONTENTS

The Core Routine

I don't like wasting a lot time and space in a book such as this one because the code in it is much more important to you than formal introductions and me blabbering on about my cat, childhood and how I got involved with perlscript.

Honestly, I'm not as important as you are.

So, here's the code that makes the rest of it work:

```
<?xml version='.o' encoding='iso-8859-1'?>
<package>
<job>
<script language="perlscript">
<![CDATA[

    package esink;

    use Win32;
    use Win32::OLE qw(in);

    my $v=0;
    my $x = 0;
    my $y = 0;

    my $rd = Win32::OLE->new("Scripting.Dictionary");
    my $nd = Win32::OLE->new("Scripting.Dictionary");


    sub OnObjectReady
    {
        local( $t ) = shift @_;
```

```perl
   local( $o) = shift @_;

   $objs = $o->Instances_(0);
   foreach $obj (in $objs)
   {
      $cd = Win32::OLE->new("Scripting.Dictionary");
      if($y eq 0)
      {
         foreach $prop (in $obj->Properties_)
         {
            $name = $prop->{Name};
            $nd->add($x, $name);
            $x = $x + 1;
         }
      }
      $cd = Win32::OLE->new("Scripting.Dictionary");
      foreach $prop (in $obj->Properties_)
      {
         $value = GetValue($prop, $obj);
         $cd->Add($x, $value);
         $x = $x + 1;
      }
      $x=0;
      $rd->Add($y, $cd);
      $y=$y+1;
   }
   WriteTheCode();
   $v=1;
}


sub OnCompleted
{
   print "Hello From OnCompleted!";
}


sub GetValue()
{

   local( $prop ) = shift @_;
   local( $obj) = shift @_;
```

```perl
        $N = $prop->{Name} . " = ";
        my $tempstr = $obj->{GetObjectText_};
        my $pos = index($tempstr, $N);
        if($pos > 0)
        {
            $pos = $pos + length($N);
            $tempstr = substr($tempstr, $pos, length($tempstr));
            $pos = index($tempstr, ";");
            $tempstr = substr($tempstr, 0, $pos);
            $tempstr =~ s/{//gi;
            $tempstr =~ s/}//gi;
            $tempstr =~ s/"//gi;
            if($prop->CIMType eq 101)
            {
                if(length($tempstr) gt 13)
                {
                    $tempstr = substr($tempstr, 4,2) . "/" . substr($tempstr, 6, 2) . "/" .
substr($tempstr, 0, 4) . " " . substr($tempstr, 8, 2) . ":" . substr($tempstr, 10, 2) .
":" . substr($tempstr, 12, 2);
                    return($tempstr);
                }
            }
            else
            {
                return($tempstr);
            }

        }
        else
        {
            return("");
        }

    }

    sub WriteTheCode()
    {


    }
```

```perl
    1;

    use strict;
    use Win32;
    use Win32::OLE qw(in EVENTS);
    Win32::OLE->Option("Warn"=>3);
    my $sink = new Win32::OLE("WbemScripting.SWbemSink");

    my $L = Win32::OLE->new("WbemScripting.SWbemLocator");
    my $svc = $L->ConnectServer(".", "root/cimv2");
    $svc->{Security_}->{AuthenticationLevel} = 6;
    $svc->{Security_}->{ImpersonationLevel} = 3;
    Win32::OLE->WithEvents($sink, "esink");
    $svc->GetAsync($sink, "Win32_Process");

    while ($v eq 0)
    {
      Win32::OLE->SpinMessageLoop();
    }
]]>
</script>
</job>
</package>
```

There's more code here doing the parsing routine than there is with the actual WbemScripting code but that's the way this works. Here's a full code example including html rendering code:

```perl
<?xml version='.0' encoding='iso-8859-1'?>
<package>
<job>
<script language="perlscript">
<![CDATA[
package esink;

use Win32;
use Win32::OLE qw(in);
```

```perl
my $v=0;
my $x = 0;
my $y = 0;

my $rd = Win32::OLE->new("Scripting.Dictionary");
my $nd = Win32::OLE->new("Scripting.Dictionary");


sub OnObjectReady
{
  local( $t ) = shift @_;
  local( $o) = shift @_;

  $objs = $o->Instances_(0);
  foreach $obj (in $objs)
  {
    $cd = Win32::OLE->new("Scripting.Dictionary");
    if($y eq 0)
    {
      foreach $prop (in $obj->Properties_)
      {
        $name = $prop->{Name};
        $nd->add($x, $name);
        $x = $x + 1;
      }
    }
    $cd = Win32::OLE >new("Scripting.Dictionary");
    foreach $prop (in $obj->Properties_)
    {
      $value = GetValue($prop, $obj);
      $cd->Add($x, $value);
      $x = $x + 1;
```

```perl
    }
    $x=0;
    $rd->Add($y, $cd);
    $y=$y+1;
  }
  WriteTheCode();
  $v=1;
}


sub OnCompleted
{
  print "Hello From OnCompleted!";
}


sub GetValue()
{

  local( $prop ) = shift @_;
  local( $obj) = shift @_;


  $N = $prop->{Name} . " = ";
  my $tempstr = $obj->{GetObjectText_};
  my $pos = index($tempstr, $N);
  if($pos > 0)
  {
    $pos = $pos + length($N);
    $tempstr = substr($tempstr, $pos, length($tempstr));
    $pos = index($tempstr, ";");
    $tempstr = substr($tempstr, 0, $pos);
    $tempstr =~ s/{//gi;
```

```perl
    $tempstr =~ s/}//gi;
    $tempstr =~ s/"//gi;
    if($prop->CIMType eq 101)
    {
        if(length($tempstr) gt 13)
        {
            $tempstr = substr($tempstr, 4,2) . "/" . substr($tempstr, 6, 2) . "/" .
substr($tempstr, 0, 4) . " " . substr($tempstr, 8, 2) . ":" . substr($tempstr, 10, 2) .
":" . substr($tempstr, 12, 2);
            return($tempstr);
        }
    }
    else
    {
        return($tempstr);
    }

}
else
{
    return("");
}

}


sub WriteTheCode()
{

    $ws = Win32::OLE->new("WScript.Shell");
    $fso = Win32::OLE->new("Scripting.FileSystemObject");
    $txtstream        =        $fso->OpenTextFile($ws->CurrentDirectory        .
"\\Win32_Process.html", 2, true, -2);
    $txtstream->WriteLine("<html>");
```

```
$txtstream->WriteLine("<head>");
$txtstream->WriteLine("<style type='text/css'>");
$txtstream->WriteLine("th");
$txtstream->WriteLine("{");
$txtstream->WriteLine("   COLOR: darkred;");
$txtstream->WriteLine("   BACKGROUND-COLOR: white;");
$txtstream->WriteLine("   FONT-FAMILY: Cambria, serif;");
$txtstream->WriteLine("   FONT-SIZE: 12px;");
$txtstream->WriteLine("   text-align: left;");
$txtstream->WriteLine("   white-Space: nowrap;");
$txtstream->WriteLine("}");
$txtstream->WriteLine("td");
$txtstream->WriteLine("{");
$txtstream->WriteLine("   COLOR: navy;");
$txtstream->WriteLine("   BACKGROUND-COLOR: white;");
$txtstream->WriteLine("   FONT-FAMILY: font-family: Cambria, serif;");
$txtstream->WriteLine("   FONT-SIZE: 12px;");
$txtstream->WriteLine("   text-align: left;");
$txtstream->WriteLine("   white-Space: nowrap;");
$txtstream->WriteLine("}");
$txtstream->WriteLine("</style>");
$txtstream->WriteLine("<title>Win32_Process</title>");
$txtstream->WriteLine("</head>");
$txtstream->WriteLine("<body>");
$txtstream->WriteLine("<table Border='2' cellpadding='3' cellspacing='3'>");
$txtstream->WriteLine("<tr>");
for($a=0; $a < length($nd->keys);$a++)
{
    $txtstream->WriteLine("<th align='left' nowrap='true'>" . $nd->items->[$a] .
"</th>");
}
$txtstream->WriteLine("</tr>");
for($z=0; $z < $y;$z++)
```

```
    {
        $txtstream->WriteLine("<tr>");
        $cd = $rd->items->[$z];
        for($a=0; $a < length($cd->keys);$a++)
        {
            $txtstream->WriteLine("<td  align='left'  nowrap='true'>" . $cd->items-
>[$a] . "</td>");
        }
        $txtstream->WriteLine("</tr>");
    }
    $txtstream->WriteLine("</tr>");
    $txtstream->WriteLine("</table>");
    $txtstream->WriteLine("</body>");
    $txtstream->WriteLine("</html>");
    $txtstream->close();

}


1;


use strict;
use Win32;
use Win32::OLE qw(in EVENTS);
Win32::OLE->Option("Warn"=>3);
my $sink = new Win32::OLE("WbemScripting.SWbemSink");

my $L = Win32::OLE->new("WbemScripting.SWbemLocator");
my $svc = $L->ConnectServer(".", "root/cimv2");
$svc->{Security_}->{AuthenticationLevel} = 6;
$svc->{Security_}->{ImpersonationLevel} = 3;
Win32::OLE->WithEvents($sink, "esink");
$svc->GetAsync($sink, "Win32_Process");
```

```
while ($v eq 0)
{
   Win32::OLE->SpinMessageLoop();
}


]]>
</script>
</job>
</package>
```

Don't know about you but when it boils down to time over effort and you can create a script like this in minutes instead of hours and you can do this for over 12,000 namespaces and classes by simply swapping out a couple of variables, you can literally create 19,200,000 different scripts. And at 100 lines per script, at 65,000 lines per year, it would take you 29538 years to write all those scripts.

Scripts, your computer can write in one week.

Anyway, just remember, when you create one of these scripts to use the ".wsf" extension instead of the ".pl" extension.

Begin Code

```
function Write_The_Code()
{
    $ws = Win32::OLE->new("WScript.Shell");
    $fso = Win32::OLE->new("Scripting.FileSystemObject");
    $txtstream = $fso->OpenTextFile($ws->CurrentDirectory .
"\\Win32_Process.html", 2, true, -2);
    $txtstream->WriteLine("<html
xmlns=\"http://www.w3.org/1999/xhtml\">");
    $txtstream->WriteLine("<head>");
    $txtstream->WriteLine("<title>Win32_Process</title>");
    $txtstream->WriteLine("</head>");
    $txtstream->WriteLine("<body>");
    $txtstream->WriteLine("<%");
    $txtstream->WriteLine("Response.Write(\"<table cellpadding=2
cellspacing=2>\" & vbcrlf)");
    $txtstream->WriteLine("Response.Write(\"<tr>\" & vbcrlf)");
    for($a=0; $a < length($nd->keys);$a ++)
    {
        $txtstream->WriteLine("Response.Write(\"<th  style='color:darkred;font-
size:10px;font-family:Cambria, serif;' align='left' nowrap>"  . $nd->items->[$a] .
"</th>\" & vbcrlf)");
    }
    $txtstream->WriteLine("Response.Write(\"</tr>\" & vbcrlf)");
```

Horizontal No Additional Tags

```
for($z=0; $z < $y;$z ++)
{
    $txtstream->WriteLine("Response.Write(\"<tr>\" & vbcrlf)");
    $cd = $rd->items->[$z];
    for($a=0; $a < length($nd->keys);$a ++)
    {
        $txtstream->WriteLine("Response.Write(\"<td   style='color:navy;font-
size:10px;font-family:Cambria, serif;' align='left' nowrap>"  . $cd->Items->[$a]  .
"</td>\" & vbcrlf)");
    }
    $txtstream->WriteLine("Response.Write(\"</tr>\" & vbcrlf)");
}
```

Horizontal Using A Button

```
for($z=0; $z < $y;$z ++)
{
    $txtstream->WriteLine("Response.Write(\"<tr>\" & vbcrlf)");
    $cd = $rd->items->[$z];
    for($a=0; $a < length($nd->keys);$a ++)
    {
        $txtstream->WriteLine("Response.Write(\"<td   style='color:navy;font-
size:10px;font-family:Cambria,  serif;'  align='left'  nowrap><input Type= button
value=\"\"  . $cd->Items->[$a] . \"\"></input></td>\" & vbcrlf)");
    }
    $txtstream->WriteLine("Response.Write(\"</tr>\" & vbcrlf)");
}
```

Horizontal Using A ComboBox

```
for($z=0; $z < $y;$z ++)
{
    $txtstream->WriteLine("Response.Write(\"<tr>\" & vbcrlf)");
```

```
        $cd = $rd->items->[$z];
        for($a=0; $a < length($nd->keys);$a ++)
        {
            $txtstream->WriteLine("Response.Write(\"<td                    style='font-
family:Calibri,        Sans-Serif;font-size:        12px;color:navy;'        align='left'
nowrap='true'><select><option value = '"   . $cd->Items->[$a]   . "'>"   . $cd-
>Items->[$a] . "</option></select></td>\" . vbcrlf)");
        }
        $txtstream->WriteLine("Response.Write(\"</tr>\" & vbcrlf)");
    }
```

Horizontal Using A Div

```
    for($z=0; $z < $y;$z ++)
    {
        $txtstream->WriteLine("Response.Write(\"<tr>\" & vbcrlf)");
        $cd = $rd->items->[$z];
        for($a=0; $a < length($nd->keys);$a ++)
        {

            $txtstream->WriteLine("Response.Write(\"<td    style='color:navy;font-
size:10px;font-family:Cambria, serif;' align='left' nowrap><div>"   . $cd->Items-
>[$a] . "</div></td>\" & vbcrlf)");

        }
        $txtstream->WriteLine("Response.Write(\"</tr>\" & vbcrlf)");
    }
```

Horizontal Using A Link

```
    for($z=0; $z < $y;$z ++)
    {
        $txtstream->WriteLine("Response.Write(\"<tr>\" & vbcrlf)");
        $cd = $rd->items->[$z];
        for($a=0; $a < length($nd->keys);$a ++)
        {
```

```
        $txtstream->WriteLine("Response.Write(\"<td      style='font-family:Calibri,
Sans-Serif;font-size: 12px;color:navy;' align='left' nowrap='true'><a href='"  . $cd-
>Items->[$a] . "'>" . $cd->Items->[$a] . "</a></td>\" . vbcrlf)");
        }
        $txtstream->WriteLine("Response.Write(\"</tr>\" & vbcrlf)");
    }
```

Horizontal Using A ListBox

```
    for(var d = 0;d < values.length;d ++
    {
        $txtstream->WriteLine("Response.Write(\"<tr>\" & vbcrlf)");
        $cd = $rd->items->[$z];
        for($a=0; $a < length($nd->keys);$a ++)
        {
            $txtstream->WriteLine("Response.Write(\"<td                    style='font-
family:Calibri,       Sans-Serif;font-size:       12px;color:navy;'       align='left'
nowrap='true'><select multiple><option value = '"  . $cd->Items->[$a]  . "'>"  .
$cd->Items->[$a] . "</option></select></td>\" . vbcrlf)");
        }
        $txtstream->WriteLine("Response.Write(\"</tr>\" & vbcrlf)");
    }
```

Horizontal Using A Span

```
    for(var d = 0;d < values.length;d ++
    {
        $txtstream->WriteLine("Response.Write(\"<tr>\" & vbcrlf)");
        $cd = $rd->items->[$z];
        for($a=0; $a < length($nd->keys);$a ++)
        {
            $txtstream->WriteLine("Response.Write(\"<td   style='color:navy;font-
size:10px;font-family:Cambria, serif;' align='left' nowrap><span>"  . $cd->Items-
>[$a] . "</span></td>\" & vbcrlf)");
        }
        $txtstream->WriteLine("Response.Write(\"</tr>\" & vbcrlf)");
    }
```

Horizontal Using A Textarea

```
for(var d = 0;d < values.length;d ++
{
    $txtstream->WriteLine("Response.Write(\"<tr>\" & vbcrlf)");
    $cd = $rd->items->[$z];
    for($a=0; $a < length($nd->keys);$a ++)
    {
        $txtstream->WriteLine("Response.Write(\"<td  style='color:navy;font-
size:10px;font-family:Cambria, serif;' align='left' nowrap><textarea>"  . $cd-
>Items->[$a] . "</textarea></td>\" & vbcrlf)");
    }
    $txtstream->WriteLine("Response.Write(\"</tr>\" & vbcrlf)");
}
```

Horizontal Using A TextBox

```
for(var d = 0;d < values.length;d ++
{
    $txtstream->WriteLine("Response.Write(\"<tr>\" & vbcrlf)");
    $cd = $rd->items->[$z];
    for($a=0; $a < length($nd->keys);$a ++)
    {
        $txtstream->WriteLine("Response.Write(\"<td  style='color:navy;font-
size:10px;font-family:Cambria, serif;' align='left' nowrap><input  Type=text
value=\"\" . $cd->Items->[$a] . \"\"></input></td>\" & vbcrlf)");

    }
    $txtstream->WriteLine("Response.Write(\"</tr>\" & vbcrlf)");
}
```

Vertical No Additional Controls

```
for($a=0; $a < length($nd->keys);$a ++)
```

```
    {
        $txtstream->WriteLine("Response.Write(\"<tr><th
style='color:darkred;font-size:10px;font-family:Cambria,       serif;'      align='left'
nowrap>" . $nd->items->[$a] . "</th>\" & vbcrlf)");
        for($z=0; $z < $y;$z ++)
        {
            $cd = $rd->items->[$z];
        $txtstream->WriteLine("Response.Write(\"<td        style='color:navy;font-
size:10px;font-family:Cambria, serif;' align='left' nowrap>" . $cd->Items->[$a] .
"</td>\" & vbcrlf)");
        }
        $txtstream->WriteLine("Response.Write(\"</tr>\" & vbcrlf)");
    }
```

Vertical Using A Button

```
    for($a=0; $a < length($nd->keys);$a ++)
    {
        $txtstream->WriteLine("Response.Write(\"<tr><th
style='color:darkred;font-size:10px;font-family:Cambria,       serif;'      align='left'
nowrap>" . $nd->items->[$a] . "</th>\" & vbcrlf)");
    for($z=0; $z < $y;$z ++)
    {
    $cd = $rd->items->[$z];
        $txtstream->WriteLine("Response.Write(\"<td        style='color:navy;font-
size:10px;font-family:Cambria, serif;' align='left' nowrap><input Type= button
value=\"\" . $cd->Items->[$a] . \"\"></input></td>\" & vbcrlf)");
    }
        $txtstream->WriteLine("Response.Write(\"</tr>\" & vbcrlf)");
    }
```

Vertical Using A ComboBox

```
    for($a=0; $a < length($nd->keys);$a ++)
    {
        $txtstream->WriteLine("Response.Write(\"<tr><th
style='color:darkred;font-size:10px;font-family:Cambria,       serif;'      align='left'
nowrap>" . $nd->items->[$a] . "</th>\" & vbcrlf)");
```

```
     for($z=0; $z < $y;$z ++)
     {
         $cd = $rd->items->[$z];
     $txtstream->WriteLine("Response.Write(\"<td        style='font-family:Calibri,
Sans-Serif;font-size: 12px;color:navy;' align='left' nowrap='true'><select><option
value  =   '''   .  $cd->Items->[$a]   .  "'>"   .  $cd->Items->[$a]   .
"</option></select></td>\" . vbcrlf)");
     }
     $txtstream->WriteLine("Response.Write(\"</tr>\" & vbcrlf)");
     }
```

Vertical Using A Div

```
     for($a=0; $a < length($nd->keys);$a ++)
     {
         $txtstream->WriteLine("Response.Write(\"<tr><th
style='color:darkred;font-size:10px;font-family:Cambria,        serif;'      align='left'
nowrap>" . $nd->items->[$a] . "</th>\" & vbcrlf)");
         for($z=0; $z < $y;$z ++)
         {
             $cd = $rd->items->[$z];
     $txtstream->WriteLine("Response.Write(\"<td           style='color:navy;font-
size:10px;font-family:Cambria, serif;' align='left' nowrap><div>"  . $cd->Items-
>[$a] . "</div></td>\" & vbcrlf)");
         }
         $txtstream->WriteLine("Response.Write(\"</tr>\" & vbcrlf)")
     }
```

Vertical Using A Link

```
     for($a=0; $a < length($nd->keys);$a ++)
     {
         $txtstream->WriteLine("Response.Write(\"<tr><th
style='color:darkred;font-size:10px;font-family:Cambria,        serif;'      align='left'
nowrap>" . $nd->items->[$a] . "</th>\" & vbcrlf)");
         for($z=0; $z < $y;$z ++)
         {
             $cd = $rd->items->[$z];
```

```
        $txtstream->WriteLine("Response.Write(\"<td        style='font-family:Calibri,
Sans-Serif;font-size: 12px;color:navy;' align='left' nowrap='true'><a href='"  . $cd-
>Items->[$a] . "'>" . $cd->Items->[$a] . "</a></td>\"  . vbcrlf)");
        }
        $txtstream->WriteLine("Response.Write(\"</tr>\"  & vbcrlf)");
    }
```

Vertical Using A ListBox

```
    for($a=0; $a < length($nd->keys);$a ++)
    {
        $txtstream->WriteLine("Response.Write(\"<tr><th
style='color:darkred;font-size:10px;font-family:Cambria,        serif;'        align='left'
nowrap>" . $nd->items->[$a] . "</th>\" & vbcrlf)");
        for($z=0; $z < $y;$z ++)
        {
            $cd = $rd->items->[$z];
            $txtstream->WriteLine("Response.Write(\"<td                style='font-
family:Calibri,        Sans-Serif;font-size:        12px;color:navy;'        align='left'
nowrap='true'><select multiple><option value = '"  . $cd->Items->[$a]  . "'>"  .
$cd->Items->[$a] . "</option></select></td>\" . vbcrlf)");
        }
        $txtstream->WriteLine("Response.Write(\"</tr>\"  & vbcrlf)");
    }
```

Vertical Using A Span

```
    for($a=0; $a < length($nd->keys);$a ++)
    {
        $txtstream->WriteLine("Response.Write(\"<tr><th
style='color:darkred;font-size:10px;font-family:Cambria,        serif;'        align='left'
nowrap>" . $nd->items->[$a] . "</th>\" & vbcrlf)");
        for($z=0; $z < $y;$z ++)
        {
            $cd = $rd->items->[$z];
        $txtstream->WriteLine("Response.Write(\"<td           style='color:navy;font-
size:10px;font-family:Cambria, serif;' align='left' nowrap><span>"  . $cd->Items-
>[$a] . "</span></td>\" & vbcrlf)");
        }
        $txtstream->WriteLine("Response.Write(\"</tr>\"  & vbcrlf)");
```

```
        }
```

Vertical Using A Textarea

```
    for($a=0; $a < length($nd->keys);$a ++)
    {
        $txtstream->WriteLine("Response.Write(\"<tr><th
style='color:darkred;font-size:10px;font-family:Cambria,        serif;'        align='left'
nowrap>" . $nd->items->[$a] . "</th>\" & vbcrlf)");
        for($z=0; $z < $y;$z ++)
        {
            $cd = $rd->items->[$z];
        $txtstream->WriteLine("Response.Write(\"<td            style='color:navy;font-
size:10px;font-family:Cambria,  serif;'  align='left'  nowrap><textarea>"   .   $cd-
>Items->[$a] . "</textarea></td>\" & vbcrlf)");
        }
        $txtstream->WriteLine("Response.Write(\"</tr>\" & vbcrlf)");
    }
```

Vertical Using A TextBox

```
    for($a=0; $a < length($nd->keys);$a ++)
    {
        $txtstream->WriteLine("Response.Write(\"<tr><th
style='color:darkred;font-size:10px;font-family:Cambria,        serif;'        align='left'
nowrap>" . $nd->items->[$a] . "</th>\" & vbcrlf)");
        for($z=0; $z < $y;$z ++)
        {
            $cd = $rd->items->[$z];
        $txtstream->WriteLine("Response.Write(\"<td            style='color:navy;font-
size:10px;font-family:Cambria,   serif;'   align='left'   nowrap><input   Type=text
value=\"\" . $cd->Items->[$a] . \"\"></input></td>\" & vbcrlf)");
        }
        $txtstream->WriteLine("Response.Write(\"</tr>\" & vbcrlf)");
    }
```

End Code

```
$txtstream->WriteLine("Response.Write(\"</table>\" & vbcrlf)");
$txtstream->WriteLine("%>");
$txtstream->WriteLine("</body>");
$txtstream->WriteLine("</html>");
$txtstream->Close();

}
```

ASP Tables

Begin Code

function Write_The_Code()

```
{
    $ws = Win32::OLE->new("WScript.Shell");
    $filename = $ws->CurrentDirectory . "\\Win32_Process.asp";
    $fso = Win32::OLE->new("Scripting.FileSystemObject");
    var txtstream = $fso->OpenTextFile(filename, 2, true, -2);
    $txtstream->WriteLine("<html
xmlns=\"http://www.w3.org/1999/xhtml\">");
    $txtstream->WriteLine("<head>");
    $txtstream->WriteLine("<title>Win32_Process</title>");
    $txtstream->WriteLine("</head>");
    $txtstream->WriteLine("<body>");
    $txtstream->WriteLine("<%");
    $txtstream->WriteLine("Response.Write(\"<table  Border=1  cellpadding=2
cellspacing=2>\" & vbcrlf)");
    $txtstream->WriteLine("Response.Write(\"<tr>\" & vbcrlf)");
    for($a=0; $a < length($nd->keys);$a ++)
    {
        $txtstream->WriteLine("Response.Write(\"<th  style='color:darkred;font-
size:10px;font-family:Cambria, serif;' align='left' nowrap>"  . $nd->items->[$a] .
"</th>\" & vbcrlf)");
    }
    $txtstream->WriteLine("Response.Write(\"</tr>\" & vbcrlf)");
```

Horizontal No Additional Tags

```
for($z=0; $z < $y;$z ++)
{
    $txtstream->WriteLine("Response.Write(\"<tr>\" & vbcrlf)");
    $cd = $rd->items->[$z];
    for($a=0; $a < length($nd->keys);$a ++)
    {
        $txtstream->WriteLine("Response.Write(\"<td  style='color:navy;font-
size:10px;font-family:Cambria, serif;' align='left' nowrap>" . $cd->Items->[$a] .
"</td>\" & vbcrlf)");
    }
    $txtstream->WriteLine("Response.Write(\"</tr>\" & vbcrlf)");
}
```

Horizontal Using A Button

```
for($z=0; $z < $y;$z ++)
{
    $txtstream->WriteLine("Response.Write(\"<tr>\" & vbcrlf)");
    $cd = $rd->items->[$z];
    for($a=0; $a < length($nd->keys);$a ++)
    {
        $txtstream->WriteLine("Response.Write(\"<td  style='color:navy;font-
size:10px;font-family:Cambria, serif;' align='left' nowrap><input Type= button
value=\"\" . $cd->Items->[$a] . \"\"></input></td>\" & vbcrlf)");
    }
    $txtstream->WriteLine("Response.Write(\"</tr>\" & vbcrlf)");
}
```

Horizontal Using A ComboBox

```
for($z=0; $z < $y;$z ++)
{
    $txtstream->WriteLine("Response.Write(\"<tr>\" & vbcrlf)");
    $cd = $rd->items->[$z];
```

```
        for($a=0; $a < length($nd->keys);$a ++)
        {
            $txtstream->WriteLine("Response.Write(\"<td                 style='font-
family:Calibri,        Sans-Serif;font-size:       12px;color:navy;'       align='left'
nowrap='true'><select><option value = '"   . $cd->Items->[$a]   . "'>"   . $cd-
>Items->[$a] . "</option></select></td>\" . vbcrlf)");
        }
        $txtstream->WriteLine("Response.Write(\"</tr>\" & vbcrlf)");
    }
```

Horizontal Using A Div

```
    for($z=0; $z < $y;$z ++)
    {
        $txtstream->WriteLine("Response.Write(\"<tr>\" & vbcrlf)");
        $cd = $rd->items->[$z];
        for($a=0; $a < length($nd->keys);$a ++)
        {

            $txtstream->WriteLine("Response.Write(\"<td    style='color:navy;font-
size:10px;font-family:Cambria, serif;' align='left' nowrap><div>"   . $cd->Items-
>[$a] . "</div></td>\" & vbcrlf)");

        }
        $txtstream->WriteLine("Response.Write(\"</tr>\" & vbcrlf)");
    }
```

Horizontal Using A Link

```
    for($z=0; $z < $y;$z ++)
    {
        $txtstream->WriteLine("Response.Write(\"<tr>\" & vbcrlf)");
        $cd = $rd->items->[$z];
        for($a=0; $a < length($nd->keys);$a ++)
        {
        $txtstream->WriteLine("Response.Write(\"<td    style='font-family:Calibri,
Sans-Serif;font-size: 12px;color:navy;' align='left' nowrap='true'><a href='"   . $cd-
>Items->[$a] . "'>" . $cd->Items->[$a] . "</a></td>\" . vbcrlf)");
```

```
        }
        $txtstream->WriteLine("Response.Write(\"</tr>\" & vbcrlf)");
    }
```

Horizontal Using A ListBox

```
    for(var d = 0;d < values.length;d ++
    {
        $txtstream->WriteLine("Response.Write(\"<tr>\" & vbcrlf)");
        $cd = $rd->items->[$z];
        for($a=0; $a < length($nd->keys);$a ++)
        {
            $txtstream->WriteLine("Response.Write(\"<td          style='font-
family:Calibri,       Sans-Serif;font-size:       12px;color:navy;'      align='left'
nowrap='true'><select multiple><option value = '"  . $cd->Items->[$a]  . "'>"  .
$cd->Items->[$a]  . "</option></select></td>\"  . vbcrlf)");
        }
        $txtstream->WriteLine("Response.Write(\"</tr>\" & vbcrlf)");
    }
```

Horizontal Using A Span

```
    for(var d = 0;d < values.length;d ++
    {
        $txtstream->WriteLine("Response.Write(\"<tr>\" & vbcrlf)");
        $cd = $rd->items->[$z];
        for($a=0; $a < length($nd->keys);$a ++)
        {
            $txtstream->WriteLine("Response.Write(\"<td   style='color:navy;font-
size:10px;font-family:Cambria, serif;' align='left' nowrap><span>"  . $cd->Items-
>[$a]  . "</span></td>\" & vbcrlf)");
        }
        $txtstream->WriteLine("Response.Write(\"</tr>\" & vbcrlf)");
    }
```

Horizontal Using A Textarea

```
for(var d = 0;d < values.length;d ++
{
    $txtstream->WriteLine("Response.Write(\"<tr>\" & vbcrlf)");
    $cd = $rd->items->[$z];
    for($a=0; $a < length($nd->keys);$a ++)
    {
        $txtstream->WriteLine("Response.Write(\"<td  style='color:navy;font-
size:10px;font-family:Cambria, serif;'  align='left'  nowrap><textarea>"  . $cd-
>Items->[$a] . "</textarea></td>\" & vbcrlf)");
    }
    $txtstream->WriteLine("Response.Write(\"</tr>\" & vbcrlf)");
}
```

Horizontal Using A TextBox

```
for(var d = 0;d < values.length;d ++
{
    $txtstream->WriteLine("Response.Write(\"<tr>\" & vbcrlf)");
    $cd = $rd->items->[$z];
    for($a=0; $a < length($nd->keys);$a ++)
    {
        $txtstream->WriteLine("Response.Write(\"<td  style='color:navy;font-
size:10px;font-family:Cambria,  serif;'  align='left'  nowrap><input  Type=text
value=\"\"  . $cd->Items->[$a] . \"\"></input></td>\" & vbcrlf)");

    }
    $txtstream->WriteLine("Response.Write(\"</tr>\" & vbcrlf)");
}
```

Vertical No Additional Controls

```
for($a=0; $a < length($nd->keys);$a ++)
{
    $txtstream->WriteLine("Response.Write(\"<tr><th
style='color:darkred;font-size:10px;font-family:Cambria,  serif;'  align='left'
nowrap>" . $nd->items->[$a] . "</th>\" & vbcrlf)");
```

```
        for($z=0; $z < $y;$z ++)
        {
            $cd = $rd->items->[$z];
    $txtstream->WriteLine("Response.Write(\"<td        style='color:navy;font-
size:10px;font-family:Cambria, serif;' align='left' nowrap>" . $cd->Items->[$a] .
"</td>\" & vbcrlf)");
        }
        $txtstream->WriteLine("Response.Write(\"</tr>\" & vbcrlf)");
    }
```

Vertical Using A Button

```
    for($a=0; $a < length($nd->keys);$a ++)
    {
        $txtstream->WriteLine("Response.Write(\"<tr><th
style='color:darkred;font-size:10px;font-family:Cambria,      serif;'      align='left'
nowrap>" . $nd->items->[$a] . "</th>\" & vbcrlf)");
    for($z=0; $z < $y;$z ++)
    {
        $cd = $rd->items->[$z];
        $txtstream->WriteLine("Response.Write(\"<td        style='color:navy;font-
size:10px;font-family:Cambria, serif;' align='left' nowrap><input Type= button
value=\"\" . $cd->Items->[$a] . \"\"></input></td>\" & vbcrlf)");
    }
        $txtstream->WriteLine("Response.Write(\"</tr>\" & vbcrlf)");
    }
```

Vertical Using A ComboBox

```
    for($a=0; $a < length($nd->keys);$a ++)
    {
        $txtstream->WriteLine("Response.Write(\"<tr><th
style='color:darkred;font-size:10px;font-family:Cambria,      serif;'      align='left'
nowrap>" . $nd->items->[$a] . "</th>\" & vbcrlf)");
        for($z=0; $z < $y;$z ++)
        {
            $cd = $rd->items->[$z];
```

```
        $txtstream->WriteLine("Response.Write(\"<td       style='font-family:Calibri,
Sans-Serif;font-size: 12px;color:navy;' align='left' nowrap='true'><select><option
value  =  '"    .  $cd->Items->[$a]    .  "'>"    .  $cd->Items->[$a]    .
"</option></select></td>\" . vbcrlf)");
        }
        $txtstream->WriteLine("Response.Write(\"</tr>\" & vbcrlf)");
    }
```

Vertical Using A Div

```
    for($a=0; $a < length($nd->keys);$a ++)
    {
        $txtstream->WriteLine("Response.Write(\"<tr><th
style='color:darkred;font-size:10px;font-family:Cambria,     serif;'     align='left'
nowrap>" . $nd->items->[$a] . "</th>\" & vbcrlf)");
        for($z=0; $z < $y;$z ++)
        {
            $cd = $rd->items->[$z];
        $txtstream->WriteLine("Response.Write(\"<td        style='color:navy;font-
size:10px;font-family:Cambria, serif;' align='left' nowrap><div>"  . $cd->Items-
>[$a] . "</div></td>\" & vbcrlf)");
        }
        $txtstream->WriteLine("Response.Write(\"</tr>\" & vbcrlf)")
    }
```

Vertical Using A Link

```
    for($a=0; $a < length($nd->keys);$a ++)
    {
        $txtstream->WriteLine("Response.Write(\"<tr><th
style='color:darkred;font-size:10px;font-family:Cambria,     serif;'     align='left'
nowrap>" . $nd->items->[$a] . "</th>\" & vbcrlf)");
        for($z=0; $z < $y;$z ++)
        {
            $cd = $rd->items->[$z];
        $txtstream->WriteLine("Response.Write(\"<td       style='font-family:Calibri,
Sans-Serif;font-size: 12px;color:navy;' align='left' nowrap='true'><a href='"  . $cd-
>Items->[$a] . "'>" . $cd->Items->[$a] . "</a></td>\" . vbcrlf)");
```

```
        }
        $txtstream->WriteLine("Response.Write(\"</tr>\" & vbcrlf)");
    }
```

Vertical Using A ListBox

```
    for($a=0; $a < length($nd->keys);$a ++)
    {
        $txtstream->WriteLine("Response.Write(\"<tr><th
style='color:darkred;font-size:10px;font-family:Cambria,     serif;'     align='left'
nowrap>" . $nd->items->[$a] . "</th>\" & vbcrlf)");
        for($z=0; $z < $y;$z ++)
        {
            $cd = $rd->items->[$z];
            $txtstream->WriteLine("Response.Write(\"<td                  style='font-
family:Calibri,     Sans-Serif;font-size:     12px;color:navy;'     align='left'
nowrap='true'><select multiple><option value = '" . $cd->Items->[$a] . "'>" .
$cd->Items->[$a] . "</option></select></td>\" . vbcrlf)");
        }
        $txtstream->WriteLine("Response.Write(\"</tr>\" & vbcrlf)");
    }
```

Vertical Using A Span

```
    for($a=0; $a < length($nd->keys);$a ++)
    {
        $txtstream->WriteLine("Response.Write(\"<tr><th
style='color:darkred;font-size:10px;font-family:Cambria,     serif;'     align='left'
nowrap>" . $nd->items->[$a] . "</th>\" & vbcrlf)");
        for($z=0; $z < $y;$z ++)
        {
            $cd = $rd->items->[$z];
        $txtstream->WriteLine("Response.Write(\"<td              style='color:navy;font-
size:10px;font-family:Cambria, serif;' align='left' nowrap><span>" . $cd->Items-
>[$a] . "</span></td>\" & vbcrlf)");
        }
        $txtstream->WriteLine("Response.Write(\"</tr>\" & vbcrlf)");
    }
```

Vertical Using A Textarea

```
    for($a=0; $a < length($nd->keys);$a ++)
    {
        $txtstream->WriteLine("Response.Write(\"<tr><th
style='color:darkred;font-size:10px;font-family:Cambria,     serif;'    align='left'
nowrap>" . $nd->items->[$a] . "</th>\" & vbcrlf)");
        for($z=0; $z < $y;$z ++)
        {
            $cd = $rd->items->[$z];
    $txtstream->WriteLine("Response.Write(\"<td        style='color:navy;font-
size:10px;font-family:Cambria,  serif;'  align='left'  nowrap><textarea>"   . $cd-
>Items->[$a] . "</textarea></td>\" & vbcrlf)");
        }
        $txtstream->WriteLine("Response.Write(\"</tr>\" & vbcrlf)");
    }
```

Vertical Using A TextBox

```
    for($a=0; $a < length($nd->keys);$a ++)
    {
        $txtstream->WriteLine("Response.Write(\"<tr><th
style='color:darkred;font-size:10px;font-family:Cambria,     serif;'    align='left'
nowrap>" . $nd->items->[$a] . "</th>\" & vbcrlf)");
        for($z=0; $z < $y;$z ++)
        {
            $cd = $rd->items->[$z];
    $txtstream->WriteLine("Response.Write(\"<td        style='color:navy;font-
size:10px;font-family:Cambria,  serif;'  align='left'  nowrap><input  Type=text
value=\"\" . $cd->Items->[$a] . \"\"></input></td>\" & vbcrlf)");
        }
        $txtstream->WriteLine("Response.Write(\"</tr>\" & vbcrlf)");
    }
```

End Code

```
    $txtstream->WriteLine("Response.Write(\"</table>\" & vbcrlf)");
```

```
$txtstream->WriteLine("%>");
$txtstream->WriteLine("</body>");
$txtstream->WriteLine("</html>");
$txtstream->Close();

}
```

Begin Code

```
$ws = Win32::OLE->new("WScript.Shell");
$filename = $ws->CurrentDirectory . "\\Win32_Process.aspx";
$fso = Win32::OLE->new("Scripting.FileSystemObject");
var txtstream = $fso->OpenTextFile(filename, 2, true, -2);
$txtstream->WriteLine("<!DOCTYPE html PUBLIC \"-//W3C//DTD XHTML
1.0    Transitional//EN\"    \"http://www.w3.org/TR/xhtml1/DTD/xhtml1-
transitional.dtd\">");
$txtstream->WriteLine("");
$txtstream->WriteLine("<html
xmlns=\"http://www.w3.org/1999/xhtml\">");
$txtstream->WriteLine("<head>");
$txtstream->WriteLine("<title>Win32_Process</title>");
$txtstream->WriteLine("</head>");
$txtstream->WriteLine("<body>");
$txtstream->WriteLine("<%");
$txtstream->WriteLine("Response.Write(\"<table         cellpadding=2
cellspacing=2>\" & vbcrlf)");
```

Horizontal Views

```
$txtstream->WriteLine("Response.Write(\"<tr>\" & vbcrlf)");
for($a=0; $a < length($nd->keys);$a ++)
{
    $txtstream->WriteLine("Response.Write(\"<th    style='color:darkred;font-
size:10px;font-family:Cambria, serif;' align='left' nowrap>" . $nd->items->[$a] .
"</th>\" & vbcrlf)");
}
$txtstream->WriteLine("Response.Write(\"</tr>\" & vbcrlf)");
```

Horizontal No Additional Tags

```
for($z=0; $z < $y;$z ++)
{
    $txtstream->WriteLine("Response.Write(\"<tr>\" & vbcrlf)");
    $cd = $rd->items->[$z];
    for($a=0; $a < length($nd->keys);$a ++)
    {
        $txtstream->WriteLine("Response.Write(\"<td   style='color:navy;font-
size:10px;font-family:Cambria, serif;' align='left' nowrap>" . $cd->Items->[$a] .
"</td>\" & vbcrlf)");
    }
    $txtstream->WriteLine("Response.Write(\"</tr>\" & vbcrlf)");
}
```

Horizontal Using A Button

```
for($z=0; $z < $y;$z ++)
{
    $txtstream->WriteLine("Response.Write(\"<tr>\" & vbcrlf)");
    $cd = $rd->items->[$z];
    for($a=0; $a < length($nd->keys);$a ++)
    {
        $txtstream->WriteLine("Response.Write(\"<td   style='color:navy;font-
size:10px;font-family:Cambria,  serif;'  align='left'  nowrap><input  Type= button
value=\"\" . $cd->Items->[$a] . \"\"></input></td>\" & vbcrlf)");
    }
    $txtstream->WriteLine("Response.Write(\"</tr>\" & vbcrlf)");
}
```

Horizontal Using A ComboBox

```
for($z=0; $z < $y;$z ++)
{
    $txtstream->WriteLine("Response.Write(\"<tr>\" & vbcrlf)");
    $cd = $rd->items->[$z];
```

```
for($a=0; $a < length($nd->keys);$a ++)
{
    $txtstream->WriteLine("Response.Write(\"<td                 style='font-
family:Calibri,      Sans-Serif;font-size:     12px;color:navy;'       align='left'
nowrap='true'><select><option value = '"  . $cd->Items->[$a]   . "'>"  . $cd-
>Items->[$a] . "</option></select></td>\" . vbcrlf)");
    }
    $txtstream->WriteLine("Response.Write(\"</tr>\" & vbcrlf)");
}
```

Horizontal Using A Div

```
for($z=0; $z < $y;$z ++)
{
    $txtstream->WriteLine("Response.Write(\"<tr>\" & vbcrlf)");
    $cd = $rd->items->[$z];
    for($a=0; $a < length($nd->keys);$a ++)
    {

        $txtstream->WriteLine("Response.Write(\"<td   style='color:navy;font-
size:10px;font-family:Cambria, serif;' align='left' nowrap><div>"   . $cd->Items-
>[$a] . "</div></td>\" & vbcrlf)");

    }
    $txtstream->WriteLine("Response.Write(\"</tr>\" & vbcrlf)");
}
```

Horizontal Using A Link

```
for($z=0; $z < $y;$z ++)
{
    $txtstream->WriteLine("Response.Write(\"<tr>\" & vbcrlf)");
    $cd = $rd->items->[$z];
    for($a=0; $a < length($nd->keys);$a ++)
    {
    $txtstream->WriteLine("Response.Write(\"<td    style='font-family:Calibri,
Sans-Serif;font-size: 12px;color:navy;' align='left' nowrap='true'><a href='"  . $cd-
>Items->[$a] . "'>" . $cd->Items->[$a] . "</a></td>\" . vbcrlf)");
```

```
        }
        $txtstream->WriteLine("Response.Write(\"</tr>\" & vbcrlf)");
    }
```

Horizontal Using A ListBox

```
    for(var d = 0;d < values.length;d ++
    {
        $txtstream->WriteLine("Response.Write(\"<tr>\" & vbcrlf)");
        $cd = $rd->items->[$z];
        for($a=0; $a < length($nd->keys);$a ++)
        {
            $txtstream->WriteLine("Response.Write(\"<td                    style='font-
family:Calibri,        Sans-Serif;font-size:    12px;color:navy;'    align='left'
nowrap='true'><select multiple><option value = '"  . $cd->Items->[$a]  . "'>"  .
$cd->Items->[$a] . "</option></select></td>\" . vbcrlf)");
        }
        $txtstream->WriteLine("Response.Write(\"</tr>\" & vbcrlf)");
    }
```

Horizontal Using A Span

```
    for(var d = 0;d < values.length;d ++
    {
        $txtstream->WriteLine("Response.Write(\"<tr>\" & vbcrlf)");
        $cd = $rd->items->[$z];
        for($a=0; $a < length($nd->keys);$a ++)
        {
            $txtstream->WriteLine("Response.Write(\"<td   style='color:navy;font-
size:10px;font-family:Cambria, serif;' align='left' nowrap><span>"  . $cd->Items-
>[$a] . "</span></td>\" & vbcrlf)");
        }
        $txtstream->WriteLine("Response.Write(\"</tr>\" & vbcrlf)");
    }
```

Horizontal Using A Textarea

```
for(var d = 0;d < values.length;d ++
{
    $txtstream->WriteLine("Response.Write(\"<tr>\" & vbcrlf)");
    $cd = $rd->items->[$z];
    for($a=0; $a < length($nd->keys);$a ++)
    {
        $txtstream->WriteLine("Response.Write(\"<td   style='color:navy;font-
size:10px;font-family:Cambria, serif;' align='left' nowrap><textarea>"   . $cd-
>Items->[$a] . "</textarea></td>\" & vbcrlf)");
    }
    $txtstream->WriteLine("Response.Write(\"</tr>\" & vbcrlf)");
}
```

Horizontal Using A TextBox

```
for(var d = 0;d < values.length;d ++
{
    $txtstream->WriteLine("Response.Write(\"<tr>\" & vbcrlf)");
    $cd = $rd->items->[$z];
    for($a=0; $a < length($nd->keys);$a ++)
    {
        $txtstream->WriteLine("Response.Write(\"<td   style='color:navy;font-
size:10px;font-family:Cambria,  serif;'  align='left'  nowrap><input   Type=text
value=\"\"  . $cd->Items->[$a] . \"\"></input></td>\" & vbcrlf)");

    }
    $txtstream->WriteLine("Response.Write(\"</tr>\" & vbcrlf)");
}
```

Vertical No Additional Controls

```
for($a=0; $a < length($nd->keys);$a ++)
{
    $txtstream->WriteLine("Response.Write(\"<tr><th
style='color:darkred;font-size:10px;font-family:Cambria,     serif;'    align='left'
nowrap>"  . $nd->items->[$a] . "</th>\" & vbcrlf)");
```

```
        for($z=0; $z < $y;$z ++)
        {
           $cd = $rd->items->[$z];
        $txtstream->WriteLine("Response.Write(\"<td        style='color:navy;font-
size:10px;font-family:Cambria, serif;' align='left' nowrap>" . $cd->Items->[$a] .
"</td>\" & vbcrlf)");
           }
        $txtstream->WriteLine("Response.Write(\"</tr>\" & vbcrlf)");
        }
```

Vertical Using A Button

```
        for($a=0; $a < length($nd->keys);$a ++)
        {
           $txtstream->WriteLine("Response.Write(\"<tr><th
style='color:darkred;font-size:10px;font-family:Cambria,    serif;'    align='left'
nowrap>" . $nd->items->[$a] . "</th>\" & vbcrlf)");
        for($z=0; $z < $y;$z ++)
        {
           $cd = $rd->items->[$z];
        $txtstream->WriteLine("Response.Write(\"<td        style='color:navy;font-
size:10px;font-family:Cambria, serif;' align='left' nowrap><input Type= button
value=\"\" . $cd->Items->[$a] . \"\"></input></td>\" & vbcrlf)");
        }
           $txtstream->WriteLine("Response.Write(\"</tr>\" & vbcrlf)");
        }
```

Vertical Using A ComboBox

```
        for($a=0; $a < length($nd->keys);$a ++)
        {
           $txtstream->WriteLine("Response.Write(\"<tr><th
style='color:darkred;font-size:10px;font-family:Cambria,    serif;'    align='left'
nowrap>" . $nd->items->[$a] . "</th>\" & vbcrlf)");
           for($z=0; $z < $y;$z ++)
           {
              $cd = $rd->items->[$z];
```

```
    $txtstream->WriteLine("Response.Write(\"<td      style='font-family:Calibri,
Sans-Serif;font-size: 12px;color:navy;' align='left' nowrap='true'><select><option
value  =  '"  .  $cd->Items->[$a]  .  "'>"  .  $cd->Items->[$a]  .
"</option></select></td>\" . vbcrlf)");
        }
    $txtstream->WriteLine("Response.Write(\"</tr>\" & vbcrlf)");
    }
```

Vertical Using A Div

```
    for($a=0; $a < length($nd->keys);$a ++)
    {
        $txtstream->WriteLine("Response.Write(\"<tr><th
style='color:darkred;font-size:10px;font-family:Cambria,    serif;'    align='left'
nowrap>" . $nd->items->[$a] . "</th>\" & vbcrlf)");
        for($z=0; $z < $y;$z ++)
        {
            $cd = $rd->items->[$z];
        $txtstream->WriteLine("Response.Write(\"<td        style='color:navy;font-
size:10px;font-family:Cambria, serif;' align='left' nowrap><div>"  . $cd->Items-
>[$a] . "</div></td>\" & vbcrlf)");
        }
        $txtstream->WriteLine("Response.Write(\"</tr>\" & vbcrlf)")
    }
```

Vertical Using A Link

```
    for($a=0; $a < length($nd->keys);$a ++)
    {
        $txtstream->WriteLine("Response.Write(\"<tr><th
style='color:darkred;font-size:10px;font-family:Cambria,    serif;'    align='left'
nowrap>" . $nd->items->[$a] . "</th>\" & vbcrlf)");
        for($z=0; $z < $y;$z ++)
        {
            $cd = $rd->items->[$z];
        $txtstream->WriteLine("Response.Write(\"<td      style='font-family:Calibri,
Sans-Serif;font-size: 12px;color:navy;' align='left' nowrap='true'><a href='"  . $cd-
>Items->[$a] . "'>" . $cd->Items->[$a] . "</a></td>\" . vbcrlf)");
```

```
        }
        $txtstream->WriteLine("Response.Write(\"</tr>\" & vbcrlf)");
    }
```

Vertical Using A ListBox

```
    for($a=0; $a < length($nd->keys);$a ++)
    {
        $txtstream->WriteLine("Response.Write(\"<tr><th
style='color:darkred;font-size:10px;font-family:Cambria,      serif;'     align='left'
nowrap>" . $nd->items->[$a] . "</th>\" & vbcrlf)");
        for($z=0; $z < $y;$z ++)
        {
            $cd = $rd->items->[$z];
            $txtstream->WriteLine("Response.Write(\"<td              style='font-
family:Calibri,      Sans-Serif;font-size:      12px;color:navy;'     align='left'
nowrap='true'><select multiple><option value = '"   . $cd->Items->[$a]  . "'>"   .
$cd->Items->[$a] . "</option></select></td>\" . vbcrlf)");
        }
        $txtstream->WriteLine("Response.Write(\"</tr>\" & vbcrlf)");
    }
```

Vertical Using A Span

```
    for($a=0; $a < length($nd->keys);$a ++)
    {
        $txtstream->WriteLine("Response.Write(\"<tr><th
style='color:darkred;font-size:10px;font-family:Cambria,      serif;'     align='left'
nowrap>" . $nd->items->[$a] . "</th>\" & vbcrlf)");
        for($z=0; $z < $y;$z ++)
        {
            $cd = $rd->items->[$z];
        $txtstream->WriteLine("Response.Write(\"<td          style='color:navy;font-
size:10px;font-family:Cambria, serif;' align='left' nowrap><span>"  . $cd->Items-
>[$a] . "</span></td>\" & vbcrlf)");
        }
        $txtstream->WriteLine("Response.Write(\"</tr>\" & vbcrlf)");
    }
```

Vertical Using A Textarea

```
for($a=0; $a < length($nd->keys);$a ++)
{
    $txtstream->WriteLine("Response.Write(\"<tr><th
style='color:darkred;font-size:10px;font-family:Cambria,    serif;'    align='left'
nowrap>" . $nd->items->[$a] . "</th>\" & vbcrlf)");
    for($z=0; $z < $y;$z ++)
    {
        $cd = $rd->items->[$z];
    $txtstream->WriteLine("Response.Write(\"<td        style='color:navy;font-
size:10px;font-family:Cambria,  serif;'  align='left'  nowrap><textarea>"    . $cd-
>Items->[$a] . "</textarea></td>\" & vbcrlf)");
    }
    $txtstream->WriteLine("Response.Write(\"</tr>\" & vbcrlf)");
}
```

Vertical Using A TextBox

```
for($a=0; $a < length($nd->keys);$a ++)
{
    $txtstream->WriteLine("Response.Write(\"<tr><th
style='color:darkred;font-size:10px;font-family:Cambria,    serif;'    align='left'
nowrap>" . $nd->items->[$a] . "</th>\" & vbcrlf)");
    for($z=0; $z < $y;$z ++)
    {
        $cd = $rd->items->[$z];
    $txtstream->WriteLine("Response.Write(\"<td        style='color:navy;font-
size:10px;font-family:Cambria,  serif;'  align='left'  nowrap><input  Type=text
value=\"\" . $cd->Items->[$a] . \"\"></input></td>\" & vbcrlf)");
    }
    $txtstream->WriteLine("Response.Write(\"</tr>\" & vbcrlf)");
}
```

End Code

```
$txtstream->WriteLine("Response.Write(\"</table>\" & vbcrlf)");
```

```
$txtstream->WriteLine("%>");
$txtstream->WriteLine("</body>");
$txtstream->WriteLine("</html>");
$txtstream->Close();

}
```

ASPX TABLES

Begin Code

```
function Write_The_Code()
{
    $ws = Win32::OLE->new("WScript.Shell");
    $filename = $ws->CurrentDirectory . "\\Win32_Process.aspx";
    $fso = Win32::OLE->new("Scripting.FileSystemObject");
    var txtstream = $fso->OpenTextFile(filename, 2, true, -2);
    $txtstream->WriteLine("<html
xmlns=\"http://www.w3.org/1999/xhtml\">");
    $txtstream->WriteLine("<head>");
    $txtstream->WriteLine("<title>Win32_Process</title>");
    $txtstream->WriteLine("</head>");
    $txtstream->WriteLine("<body>");
    $txtstream->WriteLine("<%");
    $txtstream->WriteLine("Response.Write(\"<table              cellpadding=2
cellspacing=2>\" & vbcrlf)");
    $txtstream->WriteLine("Response.Write(\"<tr>\" & vbcrlf)");
    for($a=0; $a < length($nd->keys);$a ++)
    {
        $txtstream->WriteLine("Response.Write(\"<th  style='color:darkred;font-
size:10px;font-family:Cambria, serif;' align='left' nowrap>" . $nd->items->[$a] .
"</th>\" & vbcrlf)");
    }
    $txtstream->WriteLine("Response.Write(\"</tr>\" & vbcrlf)");
```

Horizontal No Additional Tags

```
    for($z=0; $z < $y;$z ++)
    {
        $txtstream->WriteLine("Response.Write(\"<tr>\" & vbcrlf)");
        $cd = $rd->items->[$z];
        for($a=0; $a < length($nd->keys);$a ++)
        {
```

```
        $txtstream->WriteLine("Response.Write(\"<td    style='color:navy;font-
size:10px;font-family:Cambria, serif;' align='left' nowrap>" . $cd->Items->[$a] .
"</td>\" & vbcrlf)");
        }
        $txtstream->WriteLine("Response.Write(\"</tr>\" & vbcrlf)");
    }
```

Horizontal Using A Button

```
    for($z=0; $z < $y;$z ++)
    {
        $txtstream->WriteLine("Response.Write(\"<tr>\" & vbcrlf)");
        $cd = $rd->items->[$z];
        for($a=0; $a < length($nd->keys);$a ++)
        {
            $txtstream->WriteLine("Response.Write(\"<td    style='color:navy;font-
size:10px;font-family:Cambria, serif;' align='left' nowrap><input Type= button
value=\"\" . $cd->Items->[$a] . \"\"></input></td>\" & vbcrlf)");
        }
        $txtstream->WriteLine("Response.Write(\"</tr>\" & vbcrlf)");
    }
```

Horizontal Using A ComboBox

```
    for($z=0; $z < $y;$z ++)
    {
        $txtstream->WriteLine("Response.Write(\"<tr>\" & vbcrlf)");
        $cd = $rd->items->[$z];
        for($a=0; $a < length($nd->keys);$a ++)
        {
            $txtstream->WriteLine("Response.Write(\"<td              style='font-
family:Calibri,      Sans-Serif;font-size:      12px;color:navy;'       align='left'
nowrap='true'><select><option value = '" . $cd->Items->[$a] . "'>" . $cd-
>Items->[$a] . "</option></select></td>\" . vbcrlf)");
        }
        $txtstream->WriteLine("Response.Write(\"</tr>\" & vbcrlf)");
    }
```

Horizontal Using A Div

```
for($z=0; $z < $y;$z ++)
{
    $txtstream->WriteLine("Response.Write(\"<tr>\" & vbcrlf)");
    $cd = $rd->items->[$z];
    for($a=0; $a < length($nd->keys);$a ++)
    {

        $txtstream->WriteLine("Response.Write(\"<td    style='color:navy;font-
size:10px;font-family:Cambria, serif;' align='left' nowrap><div>"  . $cd->Items-
>[$a] . "</div></td>\" & vbcrlf)");

    }
    $txtstream->WriteLine("Response.Write(\"</tr>\" & vbcrlf)");
}
```

Horizontal Using A Link

```
for($z=0; $z < $y;$z ++)
{
    $txtstream->WriteLine("Response.Write(\"<tr>\" & vbcrlf)");
    $cd = $rd->items->[$z];
    for($a=0; $a < length($nd->keys);$a ++)
    {
    $txtstream->WriteLine("Response.Write(\"<td     style='font-family:Calibri,
Sans-Serif;font-size: 12px;color:navy;' align='left' nowrap='true'><a href='" . $cd-
>Items->[$a] . "'>" . $cd->Items->[$a] . "</a></td>\" . vbcrlf)");
    }
    $txtstream->WriteLine("Response.Write(\"</tr>\" & vbcrlf)");
}
```

Horizontal Using A ListBox

```
for(var d = 0;d < values.length;d ++
{

    $txtstream->WriteLine("Response.Write(\"<tr>\" & vbcrlf)");
```

```
        $cd = $rd->items->[$z];
        for($a=0; $a < length($nd->keys);$a ++)
        {
            $txtstream->WriteLine("Response.Write(\"<td                    style='font-
family:Calibri,       Sans-Serif;font-size:     12px;color:navy;'      align='left'
nowrap='true'><select multiple><option value = '"  . $cd->Items->[$a]  . "'>"  .
$cd->Items->[$a] . "</option></select></td>\" . vbcrlf)");
        }
        $txtstream->WriteLine("Response.Write(\"</tr>\" & vbcrlf)");
    }
```

Horizontal Using A Span

```
    for(var d = 0;d < values.length;d ++
    {
        $txtstream->WriteLine("Response.Write(\"<tr>\" & vbcrlf)");
        $cd = $rd->items->[$z];
        for($a=0; $a < length($nd->keys);$a ++)
        {
            $txtstream->WriteLine("Response.Write(\"<td   style='color:navy;font-
size:10px;font-family:Cambria, serif;' align='left' nowrap><span>"  . $cd->Items-
>[$a] . "</span></td>\" & vbcrlf)");
        }
        $txtstream->WriteLine("Response.Write(\"</tr>\" & vbcrlf)");
    }
```

Horizontal Using A Textarea

```
    for(var d = 0;d < values.length;d ++
    {
        $txtstream->WriteLine("Response.Write(\"<tr>\" & vbcrlf)");
        $cd = $rd->items->[$z];
        for($a=0; $a < length($nd->keys);$a ++)
        {
            $txtstream->WriteLine("Response.Write(\"<td   style='color:navy;font-
size:10px;font-family:Cambria, serif;' align='left' nowrap><textarea>"  . $cd-
>Items->[$a] . "</textarea></td>\" & vbcrlf)");
```

```
    }
    $txtstream->WriteLine("Response.Write(\"</tr>\" & vbcrlf)");
  }
```

Horizontal Using A TextBox

```
  for(var d = 0;d < values.length;d ++
  {
    $txtstream->WriteLine("Response.Write(\"<tr>\" & vbcrlf)");
    $cd = $rd->items->[$z];
    for($a=0; $a < length($nd->keys);$a ++)
    {
        $txtstream->WriteLine("Response.Write(\"<td   style='color:navy;font-size:10px;font-family:Cambria,   serif;'   align='left'   nowrap><input   Type=text value=\"\" . $cd->Items->[$a] . \"\"></input></td>\" & vbcrlf)");

    }
    $txtstream->WriteLine("Response.Write(\"</tr>\" & vbcrlf)");
  }
```

Vertical No Additional Controls

```
  for($a=0; $a < length($nd->keys);$a ++)
  {
      $txtstream->WriteLine("Response.Write(\"<tr><th style='color:darkred;font-size:10px;font-family:Cambria,       serif;'       align='left' nowrap>" . $nd->items->[$a] . "</th>\" & vbcrlf)");
      for($z=0; $z < $y;$z ++)
      {
        $cd = $rd->items->[$z];
      $txtstream->WriteLine("Response.Write(\"<td           style='color:navy;font-size:10px;font-family:Cambria, serif;' align='left' nowrap>" . $cd->Items->[$a] . "</td>\" & vbcrlf)");
      }
      $txtstream->WriteLine("Response.Write(\"</tr>\" & vbcrlf)");
  }
```

Vertical Using A Button

```
    for($a=0; $a < length($nd->keys);$a ++)
    {
        $txtstream->WriteLine("Response.Write(\"<tr><th
style='color:darkred;font-size:10px;font-family:Cambria,     serif;'     align='left'
nowrap>" . $nd->items->[$a] . "</th>\" & vbcrlf)");
    for($z=0; $z < $y;$z ++)
    {
    $cd = $rd->items->[$z];
        $txtstream->WriteLine("Response.Write(\"<td        style='color:navy;font-
size:10px;font-family:Cambria, serif;' align='left' nowrap><input Type= button
value=\"\" . $cd->Items->[$a] . \"\"></input></td>\" & vbcrlf)");
    }
        $txtstream->WriteLine("Response.Write(\"</tr>\" & vbcrlf)");
    }
```

Vertical Using A ComboBox

```
    for($a=0; $a < length($nd->keys);$a ++)
    {
        $txtstream->WriteLine("Response.Write(\"<tr><th
style='color:darkred;font-size:10px;font-family:Cambria,     serif;'     align='left'
nowrap>" . $nd->items->[$a] . "</th>\" & vbcrlf)");
        for($z=0; $z < $y;$z ++)
        {
        $cd = $rd->items->[$z];
        $txtstream->WriteLine("Response.Write(\"<td      style='font-family:Calibri,
Sans-Serif;font-size: 12px;color:navy;' align='left' nowrap='true'><select><option
value  =  '"    .   $cd->Items->[$a]    .  "'>"    .   $cd->Items->[$a]    .
"</option></select></td>\" . vbcrlf)");
        }
        $txtstream->WriteLine("Response.Write(\"</tr>\" & vbcrlf)");
    }
```

Vertical Using A Div

```
for($a=0; $a < length($nd->keys);$a ++)
{
    $txtstream->WriteLine("Response.Write(\"<tr><th
style='color:darkred;font-size:10px;font-family:Cambria,       serif;'    align='left'
nowrap>" . $nd->items->[$a] . "</th>\" & vbcrlf)");
    for($z=0; $z < $y;$z ++)
    {
        $cd = $rd->items->[$z];
    $txtstream->WriteLine("Response.Write(\"<td       style='color:navy;font-
size:10px;font-family:Cambria, serif;' align='left' nowrap><div>"  . $cd->Items-
>[$a] . "</div></td>\" & vbcrlf)");
    }
    $txtstream->WriteLine("Response.Write(\"</tr>\" & vbcrlf)")
}
```

Vertical Using A Link

```
for($a=0; $a < length($nd->keys);$a ++)
{
    $txtstream->WriteLine("Response.Write(\"<tr><th
style='color:darkred;font-size:10px;font-family:Cambria,       serif;'    align='left'
nowrap>" . $nd->items->[$a] . "</th>\" & vbcrlf)");
    for($z=0; $z < $y;$z ++)
    {
        $cd = $rd->items->[$z];
    $txtstream->WriteLine("Response.Write(\"<td      style='font-family:Calibri,
Sans-Serif;font-size: 12px;color:navy;' align='left' nowrap='true'><a href='"  . $cd-
>Items->[$a] . "'>" . $cd->Items->[$a] . "</a></td>\" . vbcrlf)");
    }
    $txtstream->WriteLine("Response.Write(\"</tr>\" & vbcrlf)");
}
```

Vertical Using A ListBox

```
for($a=0; $a < length($nd->keys);$a ++)
{
```

```
        $txtstream->WriteLine("Response.Write(\"<tr><th
style='color:darkred;font-size:10px;font-family:Cambria,    serif;'    align='left'
nowrap>" . $nd->items->[$a] . "</th>\" & vbcrlf)");
        for($z=0; $z < $y;$z ++)
        {
          $cd = $rd->items->[$z];
          $txtstream->WriteLine("Response.Write(\"<td         style='font-
family:Calibri,     Sans-Serif;font-size:    12px;color:navy;'    align='left'
nowrap='true'><select multiple><option value = '" . $cd->Items->[$a] . "'>" .
$cd->Items->[$a] . "</option></select></td>\" . vbcrlf)");
        }
        $txtstream->WriteLine("Response.Write(\"</tr>\" & vbcrlf)");
    }
```

Vertical Using A Span

```
    for($a=0; $a < length($nd->keys);$a ++)
    {
        $txtstream->WriteLine("Response.Write(\"<tr><th
style='color:darkred;font-size:10px;font-family:Cambria,    serif;'    align='left'
nowrap>" . $nd->items->[$a] . "</th>\" & vbcrlf)");
        for($z=0; $z < $y;$z ++)
        {
          $cd = $rd->items->[$z];
        $txtstream->WriteLine("Response.Write(\"<td      style='color:navy;font-
size:10px;font-family:Cambria, serif;' align='left' nowrap><span>" . $cd->Items-
>[$a] . "</span></td>\" & vbcrlf)");
        }
        $txtstream->WriteLine("Response.Write(\"</tr>\" & vbcrlf)");
    }
```

Vertical Using A Textarea

```
    for($a=0; $a < length($nd->keys);$a ++)
    {
        $txtstream->WriteLine("Response.Write(\"<tr><th
style='color:darkred;font-size:10px;font-family:Cambria,    serif;'    align='left'
nowrap>" . $nd->items->[$a] . "</th>\" & vbcrlf)");
        for($z=0; $z < $y;$z ++)
        {
          $cd = $rd->items->[$z];
```

```
    $txtstream->WriteLine("Response.Write(\"<td          style='color:navy;font-
size:10px;font-family:Cambria,   serif;'  align='left'  nowrap><textarea>"    . $cd-
>Items->[$a] . "</textarea></td>\" & vbcrlf)");
        }
        $txtstream->WriteLine("Response.Write(\"</tr>\" & vbcrlf)");
    }
```

Vertical Using A TextBox

```
    for($a=0; $a < length($nd->keys);$a ++)
    {
        $txtstream->WriteLine("Response.Write(\"<tr><th
style='color:darkred;font-size:10px;font-family:Cambria,      serif;'      align='left'
nowrap>" . $nd->items->[$a] . "</th>\" & vbcrlf)");
        for($z=0; $z < $y;$z ++)
        {
            $cd = $rd->items->[$z];
        $txtstream->WriteLine("Response.Write(\"<td          style='color:navy;font-
size:10px;font-family:Cambria,   serif;'   align='left'   nowrap><input   Type=text
value=\"\" . $cd->Items->[$a] . \"\"></input></td>\" & vbcrlf)");
        }
        $txtstream->WriteLine("Response.Write(\"</tr>\" & vbcrlf)");
    }
```

End Code

```
    $txtstream->WriteLine("Response.Write(\"</table>\" & vbcrlf)");
    $txtstream->WriteLine("%>");
    $txtstream->WriteLine("</body>");
    $txtstream->WriteLine("</html>");
    $txtstream->Close();

}
```

Begin Code

```
function Write_The_Code()
{

    $ws = Win32::OLE->new("WScript.Shell");
    $filename = $ws->CurrentDirectory . "\\Win32_Process.hta";
    $fso = Win32::OLE->new("Scripting.FileSystemObject");
    var txtstream = $fso->OpenTextFile(filename, 2, true, -2);
    $txtstream->WriteLine("<html>");
    $txtstream->WriteLine("<head>");
    $txtstream->WriteLine("<HTA:APPLICATION ");
    $txtstream->WriteLine(" ID = \"Win32_Process\" ");
    $txtstream->WriteLine(" APPLICATIONNAME = \"Win32_Process\" ");
    $txtstream->WriteLine(" SCROLL = \"Yes\" ");
    $txtstream->WriteLine(" SINGLEINSTANCE = \"yes\" ");
    $txtstream->WriteLine(" WINDOWSTATE = \"normal\">");
    $txtstream->WriteLine("<title>Win32_Process</title>");
    $txtstream->WriteLine("</head>");
    $txtstream->WriteLine("<body>");
    $txtstream->WriteLine("<table  boder=0 cellpadding=2 cellspacing=2>\" &
vbcrlf)");
```

Horizontal No Additional Tags

```
    for($z=0; $z < $y;$z ++)
```

```
    {
        $txtstream->WriteLine("<tr>\" & vbcrlf)");
        $cd = $rd->items->[$z];
        for($a=0; $a < length($nd->keys);$a ++)
        {
            $txtstream->WriteLine("<td      style='color:navy;font-size:10px;font-
family:Cambria, serif;' align='left' nowrap>" . $cd->Items->[$a] . "</td>");
        }
        $txtstream->WriteLine("</tr>");
    }
```

Horizontal Using A Button

```
    for($z=0; $z < $y;$z ++)
    {
        $txtstream->WriteLine("<tr>");
        $cd = $rd->items->[$z];
        for($a=0; $a < length($nd->keys);$a ++)
        {
            $txtstream->WriteLine("<td      style='color:navy;font-size:10px;font-
family:Cambria, serif;' align='left' nowrap><input Type= button value=\"\" . $cd-
>Items->[$a] . \"\"></input></td>");
        }
        $txtstream->WriteLine("</tr>");
    }
```

Horizontal Using A ComboBox

```
    for($z=0; $z < $y;$z ++)
    {
        $txtstream->WriteLine("<tr>");
        $cd = $rd->items->[$z];
        for($a=0; $a < length($nd->keys);$a ++)
        {
            $txtstream->WriteLine("<td      style='font-family:Calibri,      Sans-
Serif;font-size: 12px;color:navy;' align='left' nowrap='true'><select><option value =
```

```
'" . $cd->Items->[$a] . "'>" . $cd->Items->[$a] . "</option></select></td>\" .
vbcrlf)");
        }
        $txtstream->WriteLine("</tr>");
    }
```

Horizontal Using A Div

```
    for($z=0; $z < $y;$z ++)
    {
        $txtstream->WriteLine("<tr>");
        $cd = $rd->items->[$z];
        for($a=0; $a < length($nd->keys);$a ++)
        {

            $txtstream->WriteLine("<td        style='color:navy;font-size:10px;font-
family:Cambria,  serif;'  align='left'  nowrap><div>"    .  $cd->Items->[$a]    .
"</div></td>");

        }
        $txtstream->WriteLine("</tr>");
    }
```

Horizontal Using A Link

```
    for($z=0; $z < $y;$z ++)
    {
        $txtstream->WriteLine("<tr>");
        $cd = $rd->items->[$z];
        for($a=0; $a < length($nd->keys);$a ++)
        {
        $txtstream->WriteLine("<td style='font-family:Calibri, Sans-Serif;font-size:
12px;color:navy;' align='left' nowrap='true'><a href='" . $cd->Items->[$a] . "'>" .
$cd->Items->[$a] . "</a></td>\" . vbcrlf)");
        }
        $txtstream->WriteLine("</tr>");
    }
```

Horizontal Using A ListBox

```
for(var d = 0;d < values.length;d ++
{
    $txtstream->WriteLine("<tr>");
    $cd = $rd->items->[$z];
    for($a=0; $a < length($nd->keys);$a ++)
    {
        $txtstream->WriteLine("<td        style='font-family:Calibri,      Sans-
Serif;font-size:      12px;color:navy;'      align='left'      nowrap='true'><select
multiple><option value = '"   . $cd->Items->[$a]   . "'>"   . $cd->Items->[$a]   .
"</option></select></td>\"  . vbcrlf)");
    }
    $txtstream->WriteLine("</tr>");
}
```

Horizontal Using A Span

```
for(var d = 0;d < values.length;d ++
{
    $txtstream->WriteLine("<tr>");
    $cd = $rd->items->[$z];
    for($a=0; $a < length($nd->keys);$a ++)
    {
        $txtstream->WriteLine("<td        style='color:navy;font-size:10px;font-
family:Cambria,  serif;'  align='left'  nowrap><span>"    . $cd->Items->[$a]    .
"</span></td>");
    }
    $txtstream->WriteLine("</tr>");
}
```

Horizontal Using A Textarea

```
for(var d = 0;d < values.length;d ++
{
    $txtstream->WriteLine("<tr>");
```

```
        $cd = $rd->items->[$z];
        for($a=0; $a < length($nd->keys);$a ++)
        {
            $txtstream->WriteLine("<td        style='color:navy;font-size:10px;font-
family:Cambria, serif;' align='left' nowrap><textarea>"  . $cd->Items->[$a]   .
"</textarea></td>");
        }
        $txtstream->WriteLine("</tr>");
    }
```

Horizontal Using A TextBox

```
    for(var d = 0;d < values.length;d ++
    {
        $txtstream->WriteLine("<tr>");
        $cd = $rd->items->[$z];
        for($a=0; $a < length($nd->keys);$a ++)
        {
            $txtstream->WriteLine("<td        style='color:navy;font-size:10px;font-
family:Cambria, serif;' align='left' nowrap><input Type=text value=\"\"   . $cd-
>Items->[$a]  . \"\"></input></td>");

        }
        $txtstream->WriteLine("</tr>");
    }
```

Vertical No Additional Controls

```
    for($a=0; $a < length($nd->keys);$a ++)
    {
        $txtstream->WriteLine("<tr><th                style='color:darkred;font-
size:10px;font-family:Cambria, serif;' align='left' nowrap>"  . $nd->items->[$a] .
"</th>");
        for($z=0; $z < $y;$z ++)
        {
            $cd = $rd->items->[$z];
```

```
        $txtstream->WriteLine("<td            style='color:navy;font-size:10px;font-
family:Cambria, serif;' align='left' nowrap>" . $cd->Items->[$a] . "</td>");
        }
        $txtstream->WriteLine("</tr>");
    }
```

Vertical Using A Button

```
    for($a=0; $a < length($nd->keys);$a ++)
    {
        $txtstream->WriteLine("<tr><th                style='color:darkred;font-
size:10px;font-family:Cambria, serif;' align='left' nowrap>" . $nd->items->[$a] .
"</th>");
    for($z=0; $z < $y;$z ++)
    {
        $cd = $rd->items->[$z];
        $txtstream->WriteLine("<td           style='color:navy;font-size:10px;font-
family:Cambria, serif;' align='left' nowrap><input Type= button value=\"\" . $cd-
>Items->[$a] . \"\"></input></td>");
    }
        $txtstream->WriteLine("</tr>");
    }
```

Vertical Using A ComboBox

```
    for($a=0; $a < length($nd->keys);$a ++)
    {
        $txtstream->WriteLine("<tr><th                style='color:darkred;font-
size:10px;font-family:Cambria, serif;' align='left' nowrap>" . $nd->items->[$a] .
"</th>");
        for($z=0; $z < $y;$z ++)
        {
            $cd = $rd->items->[$z];
        $txtstream->WriteLine("<td style='font-family:Calibri, Sans-Serif;font-size:
12px;color:navy;' align='left' nowrap='true'><select><option value = '" . $cd-
>Items->[$a] . "'>" . $cd->Items->[$a] . "</option></select></td>\" . vbcrlf)");
        }
        $txtstream->WriteLine("</tr>");
```

```
        }
```

Vertical Using A Div

```
    for($a=0; $a < length($nd->keys);$a ++)
    {
        $txtstream->WriteLine("<tr><th                style='color:darkred;font-
size:10px;font-family:Cambria, serif;' align='left' nowrap>" . $nd->items->[$a] .
"</th>");
        for($z=0; $z < $y;$z ++)
        {
          $cd = $rd->items->[$z];
        $txtstream->WriteLine("<td            style='color:navy;font-size:10px;font-
family:Cambria,  serif;' align='left'  nowrap><div>"  . $cd->Items->[$a]   .
"</div></td>");
        }
        $txtstream->WriteLine("</tr>")
    }
```

Vertical Using A Link

```
    for($a=0; $a < length($nd->keys);$a ++)
    {
        $txtstream->WriteLine("<tr><th                style='color:darkred;font-
size:10px;font-family:Cambria, serif;' align='left' nowrap>" . $nd->items->[$a] .
"</th>");
        for($z=0; $z < $y;$z ++)
        {
          $cd = $rd->items->[$z];
        $txtstream->WriteLine("<td style='font-family:Calibri, Sans-Serif;font-size:
12px;color:navy;' align='left' nowrap='true'><a href='" . $cd->Items->[$a] . "'>" .
$cd->Items->[$a] . "</a></td>\" . vbcrlf)");
        }
        $txtstream->WriteLine("</tr>");
    }
```

Vertical Using A ListBox

```
for($a=0; $a < length($nd->keys);$a ++)
{
    $txtstream->WriteLine("<tr><th                style='color:darkred;font-
size:10px;font-family:Cambria, serif;' align='left' nowrap>"  . $nd->items->[$a] .
"</th>");
        for($z=0; $z < $y;$z ++)
        {
          $cd = $rd->items->[$z];
          $txtstream->WriteLine("<td        style='font-family:Calibri,      Sans-
Serif;font-size:       12px;color:navy;'      align='left'      nowrap='true'><select
multiple><option value = '"   . $cd->Items->[$a]  . "'>"   . $cd->Items->[$a]  .
"</option></select></td>\"  . vbcrlf)");
        }
    $txtstream->WriteLine("</tr>");
}
```

Vertical Using A Span

```
for($a=0; $a < length($nd->keys);$a ++)
{
    $txtstream->WriteLine("<tr><th                style='color:darkred;font-
size:10px;font-family:Cambria, serif;' align='left' nowrap>"  . $nd->items->[$a] .
"</th>");
        for($z=0; $z < $y;$z ++)
        {
          $cd = $rd->items->[$z];
      $txtstream->WriteLine("<td           style='color:navy;font-size:10px;font-
family:Cambria, serif;' align='left' nowrap><span>"   . $cd->Items->[$a]    .
"</span></td>");
        }
    $txtstream->WriteLine("</tr>");
}
```

Vertical Using A Textarea

```
for($a=0; $a < length($nd->keys);$a ++)
{
    $txtstream->WriteLine("<tr><th                style='color:darkred;font-
size:10px;font-family:Cambria, serif;' align='left' nowrap>"  . $nd->items->[$a] .
"</th>");
        for($z=0; $z < $y;$z ++)
```

```
        {
            $cd = $rd->items->[$z];
        $txtstream->WriteLine("<td                style='color:navy;font-size:10px;font-
family:Cambria,  serif;'  align='left'  nowrap><textarea>"    .  $cd->Items->[$a]    .
"</textarea></td>");
            }
        $txtstream->WriteLine("</tr>");
    }
```

Vertical Using A TextBox

```
    for($a=0; $a < length($nd->keys);$a ++)
    {
        $txtstream->WriteLine("<tr><th                   style='color:darkred;font-
size:10px;font-family:Cambria,  serif;'  align='left'  nowrap>"  .  $nd->items->[$a] .
"</th>");
        for($z=0; $z < $y;$z ++)
        {
            $cd = $rd->items->[$z];
        $txtstream->WriteLine("<td                style='color:navy;font-size:10px;font-
family:Cambria,  serif;'  align='left'  nowrap><input Type=text value=\"\"   . $cd-
>Items->[$a]  . \"\"></input></td>");
            }
        $txtstream->WriteLine("</tr>");
    }
```

End Code

```
    $txtstream->WriteLine("</table>");
    $txtstream->WriteLine("</body>");
    $txtstream->WriteLine("</html>");
    $txtstream->Close();
}
```

HTA TABLES

Begin Code

```
function Write_The_Code()
{

    $ws = Win32::OLE->new("WScript.Shell");
    $filename = $ws->CurrentDirectory . "\\Win32_Process.hta";
    $fso = Win32::OLE->new("Scripting.FileSystemObject");
    var txtstream = $fso->OpenTextFile(filename, 2, true, -2);
    $txtstream->WriteLine("<html>");
    $txtstream->WriteLine("<head>");
    $txtstream->WriteLine("<HTA:APPLICATION ");
    $txtstream->WriteLine(" ID = \"Win32_Process\" ");
    $txtstream->WriteLine(" APPLICATIONNAME = \"Win32_Process\" ");
    $txtstream->WriteLine(" SCROLL = \"Yes\" ");
    $txtstream->WriteLine(" SINGLEINSTANCE = \"yes\" ");
    $txtstream->WriteLine(" WINDOWSTATE = \"normal\">");
    $txtstream->WriteLine("<title>Win32_Process</title>");
    $txtstream->WriteLine("</head>");
    $txtstream->WriteLine("<body>");
    $txtstream->WriteLine("<table boder=1 cellpadding=2 cellspacing=2>");
```

Horizontal No Additional Tags

```
for($z=0; $z < $y;$z ++)
{
    $txtstream->WriteLine("<tr>");
    $cd = $rd->items->[$z];
    for($a=0; $a < length($nd->keys);$a ++)
    {
        $txtstream->WriteLine("<td        style='color:navy;font-size:10px;font-
family:Cambria, serif;' align='left' nowrap>" . $cd->Items->[$a] . "</td>");
    }
    $txtstream->WriteLine("</tr>");
}
```

Horizontal Using A Button

```
for($z=0; $z < $y;$z ++)
{
    $txtstream->WriteLine("<tr>");
    $cd = $rd->items->[$z];
    for($a=0; $a < length($nd->keys);$a ++)
    {
        $txtstream->WriteLine("<td        style='color:navy;font-size:10px;font-
family:Cambria, serif;' align='left' nowrap><input Type= button value=\"\" . $cd-
>Items->[$a] . \"\"></input></td>");
    }
    $txtstream->WriteLine("</tr>");
}
```

Horizontal Using A ComboBox

```
for($z=0; $z < $y;$z ++)
{
    $txtstream->WriteLine("<tr>");
    $cd = $rd->items->[$z];
    for($a=0; $a < length($nd->keys);$a ++)
```

```
      {
          $txtstream->WriteLine("<td        style='font-family:Calibri,     Sans-
Serif;font-size: 12px;color:navy;' align='left' nowrap='true'><select><option value =
'" . $cd->Items->[$a] . "'>" . $cd->Items->[$a] . "</option></select></td>\" .
vbcrlf)");
      }
      $txtstream->WriteLine("</tr>");
   }
```

Horizontal Using A Div

```
   for($z=0; $z < $y;$z ++)
   {
      $txtstream->WriteLine("<tr>");
      $cd = $rd->items->[$z];
      for($a=0; $a < length($nd->keys);$a ++)
      {

          $txtstream->WriteLine("<td       style='color:navy;font-size:10px;font-
family:Cambria,  serif;'  align='left'  nowrap><div>"    .  $cd->Items->[$a]    .
"</div></td>");

      }
      $txtstream->WriteLine("</tr>");
   }
```

Horizontal Using A Link

```
   for($z=0; $z < $y;$z ++)
   {
      $txtstream->WriteLine("<tr>");
      $cd = $rd->items->[$z];
      for($a=0; $a < length($nd->keys);$a ++)
      {
      $txtstream->WriteLine("<td style='font-family:Calibri, Sans-Serif;font-size:
12px;color:navy;' align='left' nowrap='true'><a href='" . $cd->Items->[$a] . "'>" .
$cd->Items->[$a] . "</a></td>\" . vbcrlf)");
      }
```

```
$txtstream->WriteLine("</tr>");
    }
```

Horizontal Using A ListBox

```
for(var d = 0;d < values.length;d ++
    {
    $txtstream->WriteLine("<tr>");
    $cd = $rd->items->[$z];
    for($a=0; $a < length($nd->keys);$a ++)
        {
        $txtstream->WriteLine("<td        style='font-family:Calibri,        Sans-
Serif;font-size:    12px;color:navy;'        align='left'        nowrap='true'><select
multiple><option value = '"  . $cd->Items->[$a]  . "'>"  . $cd->Items->[$a]  .
"</option></select></td>\"  . vbcrlf)");
        }
    $txtstream->WriteLine("</tr>");
    }
```

Horizontal Using A Span

```
for(var d = 0;d < values.length;d ++
    {
    $txtstream->WriteLine("<tr>");
    $cd = $rd->items->[$z];
    for($a=0; $a < length($nd->keys);$a ++)
        {
        $txtstream->WriteLine("<td        style='color:navy;font-size:10px;font-
family:Cambria,  serif;'  align='left'  nowrap><span>"    . $cd->Items->[$a]    .
"</span></td>");
        }
    $txtstream->WriteLine("</tr>");
    }
```

Horizontal Using A Textarea

```
for(var d = 0;d < values.length;d ++
{
    $txtstream->WriteLine("<tr>");
    $cd = $rd->items->[$z];
    for($a=0; $a < length($nd->keys);$a ++)
    {
        $txtstream->WriteLine("<td       style='color:navy;font-size:10px;font-
family:Cambria, serif;' align='left' nowrap><textarea>"   . $cd->Items->[$a]    .
"</textarea></td>");
    }
    $txtstream->WriteLine("</tr>");
}
```

Horizontal Using A TextBox

```
for(var d = 0;d < values.length;d ++
{
    $txtstream->WriteLine("<tr>");
    $cd = $rd->items->[$z];
    for($a=0; $a < length($nd->keys);$a ++)
    {
        $txtstream->WriteLine("<td       style='color:navy;font-size:10px;font-
family:Cambria, serif;' align='left' nowrap><input Type=text value=\"\"   . $cd-
>Items->[$a] . \"\"></input></td>");

    }
    $txtstream->WriteLine("</tr>");
}
```

Vertical No Additional Controls

```
for($a=0; $a < length($nd->keys);$a ++)
{
    $txtstream->WriteLine("<tr><th                style='color:darkred;font-
size:10px;font-family:Cambria, serif;' align='left' nowrap>"   . $nd->items->[$a] .
"</th>");
```

```
        for($z=0; $z < $y;$z ++)
        {
            $cd = $rd->items->[$z];
        $txtstream->WriteLine("<td            style='color:navy;font-size:10px;font-
family:Cambria, serif;' align='left' nowrap>" . $cd->Items->[$a] . "</td>");
        }
        $txtstream->WriteLine("</tr>");
    }
```

Vertical Using A Button

```
    for($a=0; $a < length($nd->keys);$a ++)
    {
        $txtstream->WriteLine("<tr><th                style='color:darkred;font-
size:10px;font-family:Cambria, serif;' align='left' nowrap>" . $nd->items->[$a] .
"</th>");
    for($z=0; $z < $y;$z ++)
    {
        $cd = $rd->items->[$z];
        $txtstream->WriteLine("<td            style='color:navy;font-size:10px;font-
family:Cambria, serif;' align='left' nowrap><input Type= button value=\"\" . $cd-
>Items->[$a] .\"\"></input></td>");
    }
        $txtstream->WriteLine("</tr>");
    }
```

Vertical Using A ComboBox

```
    for($a=0; $a < length($nd->keys);$a ++)
    {
        $txtstream->WriteLine("<tr><th                style='color:darkred;font-
size:10px;font-family:Cambria, serif;' align='left' nowrap>" . $nd->items->[$a] .
"</th>");
        for($z=0; $z < $y;$z ++)
        {
            $cd = $rd->items->[$z];
```

```
$txtstream->WriteLine("<td style='font-family:Calibri, Sans-Serif;font-size:
12px;color:navy;' align='left' nowrap='true'><select><option value = '"   . $cd-
>Items->[$a] . "'>" . $cd->Items->[$a] . "</option></select></td>\" . vbcrlf)");
        }
        $txtstream->WriteLine("</tr>");
    }
```

Vertical Using A Div

```
    for($a=0; $a < length($nd->keys);$a ++)
    {
        $txtstream->WriteLine("<tr><th                 style='color:darkred;font-
size:10px;font-family:Cambria, serif;' align='left' nowrap>"  . $nd->items->[$a] .
"</th>");
        for($z=0; $z < $y;$z ++)
        {
          $cd = $rd->items->[$z];
        $txtstream->WriteLine("<td              style='color:navy;font-size:10px;font-
family:Cambria, serif;' align='left' nowrap><div>"   . $cd->Items->[$a]    .
"</div></td>");
        }
        $txtstream->WriteLine("</tr>")
    }
```

Vertical Using A Link

```
    for($a=0; $a < length($nd->keys);$a ++)
    {
        $txtstream->WriteLine("<tr><th                 style='color:darkred;font-
size:10px;font-family:Cambria, serif;' align='left' nowrap>"  . $nd->items->[$a] .
"</th>");
        for($z=0; $z < $y;$z ++)
        {
          $cd = $rd->items->[$z];
        $txtstream->WriteLine("<td style='font-family:Calibri, Sans-Serif;font-size:
12px;color:navy;' align='left' nowrap='true'><a href='"  . $cd->Items->[$a] . "'>" .
$cd->Items->[$a] . "</a></td>\" . vbcrlf)");
        }
        $txtstream->WriteLine("</tr>");
```

```
        }
```

Vertical Using A ListBox

```
    for($a=0; $a < length($nd->keys);$a ++)
    {
        $txtstream->WriteLine("<tr><th                style='color:darkred;font-
size:10px;font-family:Cambria, serif;' align='left' nowrap>" . $nd->items->[$a] .
"</th>");
        for($z=0; $z < $y;$z ++)
        {
          $cd = $rd->items->[$z];
            $txtstream->WriteLine("<td        style='font-family:Calibri,        Sans-
Serif;font-size:     12px;color:navy;'      align='left'       nowrap='true'><select
multiple><option value = '"  . $cd->Items->[$a]  . "'>"  . $cd->Items->[$a]  .
"</option></select></td>\" . vbcrlf)");
        }
        $txtstream->WriteLine("</tr>");
    }
```

Vertical Using A Span

```
    for($a=0; $a < length($nd->keys);$a ++)
    {
        $txtstream->WriteLine("<tr><th                style='color:darkred;font-
size:10px;font-family:Cambria, serif;' align='left' nowrap>" . $nd->items->[$a] .
"</th>");
        for($z=0; $z < $y;$z ++)
        {
          $cd = $rd->items->[$z];
        $txtstream->WriteLine("<td            style='color:navy;font-size:10px;font-
family:Cambria, serif;' align='left' nowrap><span>"   . $cd->Items->[$a]   .
"</span></td>");
        }
        $txtstream->WriteLine("</tr>");
    }
```

Vertical Using A Textarea

```
    for($a=0; $a < length($nd->keys);$a ++)
```

```
    {
        $txtstream->WriteLine("<tr><th                style='color:darkred;font-
size:10px;font-family:Cambria, serif;' align='left' nowrap>" . $nd->items->[$a] .
"</th>");
        for($z=0; $z < $y;$z ++)
        {
            $cd = $rd->items->[$z];
        $txtstream->WriteLine("<td              style='color:navy;font-size:10px;font-
family:Cambria, serif;' align='left' nowrap><textarea>"   . $cd->Items->[$a]   .
"</textarea></td>");
        }
        $txtstream->WriteLine("</tr>");
    }
```

Vertical Using A TextBox

```
    for($a=0; $a < length($nd->keys);$a ++)
    {
        $txtstream->WriteLine("<tr><th                style='color:darkred;font-
size:10px;font-family:Cambria, serif;' align='left' nowrap>" . $nd->items->[$a] .
"</th>");
        for($z=0; $z < $y;$z ++)
        {
            $cd = $rd->items->[$z];
        $txtstream->WriteLine("<td              style='color:navy;font-size:10px;font-
family:Cambria, serif;' align='left' nowrap><input Type=text value=\"\"   . $cd-
>Items->[$a] . \"\"></input></td>");
        }
        $txtstream->WriteLine("</tr>");
    }
```

End Code

```
    $txtstream->WriteLine("</table>");
    $txtstream->WriteLine("</body>");
    $txtstream->WriteLine("</html>");
    $txtstream->Close();
}
```

HTML REPORTS

Begin Code

```
function Write_The_Code()
{

    $ws = Win32::OLE->new("WScript.Shell");
    $filename = $ws->CurrentDirectory . "\\Win32_Process.hta";
    $fso = Win32::OLE->new("Scripting.FileSystemObject");
    var txtstream = $fso->OpenTextFile(filename, 2, true, -2);
    $txtstream->WriteLine("<html>");
    $txtstream->WriteLine("<head>");
    $txtstream->WriteLine("<title>Win32_Process</title>");
    $txtstream->WriteLine("</head>");
    $txtstream->WriteLine("<body>");
    $txtstream->WriteLine("<table  boder=0 cellpadding=2 cellspacing=2>");
```

Horizontal No Additional Tags

```
for($z=0; $z < $y;$z ++)
{
    $txtstream->WriteLine("<tr>");
    $cd = $rd->items->[$z];
    for($a=0; $a < length($nd->keys);$a ++)
    {
        $txtstream->WriteLine("<td        style='color:navy;font-size:10px;font-
family:Cambria, serif;' align='left' nowrap>" . $cd->Items->[$a] . "</td>");
    }
    $txtstream->WriteLine("</tr>");
}
```

Horizontal Using A Button

```
for($z=0; $z < $y;$z ++)
{
    $txtstream->WriteLine("<tr>");
    $cd = $rd->items->[$z];
    for($a=0; $a < length($nd->keys);$a ++)
    {
        $txtstream->WriteLine("<td        style='color:navy;font-size:10px;font-
family:Cambria, serif;' align='left' nowrap><input Type= button value=\"\" . $cd-
>Items->[$a] . \"\"></input></td>");
    }
    $txtstream->WriteLine("</tr>");
}
```

Horizontal Using A ComboBox

```
for($z=0; $z < $y;$z ++)
{
    $txtstream->WriteLine("<tr>");
    $cd = $rd->items->[$z];
    for($a=0; $a < length($nd->keys);$a ++)
```

```
        {
            $txtstream->WriteLine("<td          style='font-family:Calibri,          Sans-
Serif;font-size: 12px;color:navy;' align='left' nowrap='true'><select><option value =
'" . $cd->Items->[$a] . "'>" . $cd->Items->[$a] . "</option></select></td>\"  .
vbcrlf)");
        }
        $txtstream->WriteLine("</tr>");
    }
```

Horizontal Using A Div

```
    for($z=0; $z < $y;$z ++)
    {
        $txtstream->WriteLine("<tr>");
        $cd = $rd->items->[$z];
        for($a=0; $a < length($nd->keys);$a ++)
        {

            $txtstream->WriteLine("<td          style='color:navy;font-size:10px;font-
family:Cambria,  serif;'  align='left'  nowrap><div>"    .  $cd->Items->[$a]    .
"</div></td>");

        }
        $txtstream->WriteLine("</tr>");
    }
```

Horizontal Using A Link

```
    for($z=0; $z < $y;$z ++)
    {
        $txtstream->WriteLine("<tr>");
        $cd = $rd->items->[$z];
        for($a=0; $a < length($nd->keys);$a ++)
        {
        $txtstream->WriteLine("<td style='font-family:Calibri, Sans-Serif;font-size:
12px;color:navy;' align='left' nowrap='true'><a href='" . $cd->Items->[$a] . "'>" .
$cd->Items->[$a] . "</a></td>\" . vbcrlf)");
        }
```

```
$txtstream->WriteLine("</tr>");
  }
```

Horizontal Using A ListBox

```
for(var d = 0;d < values.length;d ++
  {
    $txtstream->WriteLine("<tr>");
    $cd = $rd->items->[$z];
    for($a=0; $a < length($nd->keys);$a ++)
    {
        $txtstream->WriteLine("<td        style='font-family:Calibri,      Sans-
Serif;font-size:      12px;color:navy;'        align='left'        nowrap='true'><select
multiple><option value = '"  . $cd->Items->[$a]  . "'>"  . $cd->Items->[$a]  .
"</option></select></td>\"  . vbcrlf)");
    }
    $txtstream->WriteLine("</tr>");
  }
```

Horizontal Using A Span

```
for(var d = 0;d < values.length;d ++
  {
    $txtstream->WriteLine("<tr>");
    $cd = $rd->items->[$z];
    for($a=0; $a < length($nd->keys);$a ++)
    {
        $txtstream->WriteLine("<td        style='color:navy;font-size:10px;font-
family:Cambria,  serif;'  align='left'  nowrap><span>"    . $cd->Items->[$a]    .
"</span></td>");
    }
    $txtstream->WriteLine("</tr>");
  }
```

Horizontal Using A Textarea

```
for(var d = 0;d < values.length;d ++
{
    $txtstream->WriteLine("<tr>");
    $cd = $rd->items->[$z];
    for($a=0; $a < length($nd->keys);$a ++)
    {
        $txtstream->WriteLine("<td       style='color:navy;font-size:10px;font-
family:Cambria, serif;' align='left' nowrap><textarea>" . $cd->Items->[$a]   .
"</textarea></td>");
    }
    $txtstream->WriteLine("</tr>");
}
```

Horizontal Using A TextBox

```
for(var d = 0;d < values.length;d ++
{
    $txtstream->WriteLine("<tr>");
    $cd = $rd->items->[$z];
    for($a=0; $a < length($nd->keys);$a ++)
    {
        $txtstream->WriteLine("<td       style='color:navy;font-size:10px;font-
family:Cambria, serif;' align='left' nowrap><input Type=text value=\"\"   . $cd-
>Items->[$a] . \"\"></input></td>");

    }
    $txtstream->WriteLine("</tr>");
}
```

Vertical No Additional Controls

```
for($a=0; $a < length($nd->keys);$a ++)
{
    $txtstream->WriteLine("<tr><th               style='color:darkred;font-
size:10px;font-family:Cambria, serif;' align='left' nowrap>" . $nd->items->[$a] .
"</th>");
```

```
    for($z=0; $z < $y;$z ++)
    {
        $cd = $rd->items->[$z];
$txtstream->WriteLine("<td            style='color:navy;font-size:10px;font-
family:Cambria, serif;' align='left' nowrap>" . $cd->Items->[$a] . "</td>");
    }
    $txtstream->WriteLine("</tr>");
}
```

Vertical Using A Button

```
    for($a=0; $a < length($nd->keys);$a ++)
    {
        $txtstream->WriteLine("<tr><th                style='color:darkred;font-
size:10px;font-family:Cambria, serif;' align='left' nowrap>"  . $nd->items->[$a] .
"</th>");
    for($z=0; $z < $y;$z ++)
    {
        $cd = $rd->items->[$z];
        $txtstream->WriteLine("<td         style='color:navy;font-size:10px;font-
family:Cambria, serif;' align='left' nowrap><input Type= button value=\"\"  . $cd-
>Items->[$a] . \"\"></input></td>");
    }
        $txtstream->WriteLine("</tr>");
    }
```

Vertical Using A ComboBox

```
    for($a=0; $a < length($nd->keys);$a ++)
    {
        $txtstream->WriteLine("<tr><th                style='color:darkred;font-
size:10px;font-family:Cambria, serif;' align='left' nowrap>"  . $nd->items->[$a] .
"</th>");
        for($z=0; $z < $y;$z ++)
        {
            $cd = $rd->items->[$z];
```

```
    $txtstream->WriteLine("<td style='font-family:Calibri, Sans-Serif;font-size:
12px;color:navy;' align='left' nowrap='true'><select><option value = '"   . $cd-
>Items->[$a] . "'>" . $cd->Items->[$a] . "</option></select></td>\" . vbcrlf)");
    }
    $txtstream->WriteLine("</tr>");
  }
```

Vertical Using A Div

```
    for($a=0; $a < length($nd->keys);$a ++)
    {
      $txtstream->WriteLine("<tr><th              style='color:darkred;font-
size:10px;font-family:Cambria, serif;' align='left' nowrap>"   . $nd->items->[$a] .
"</th>");
        for($z=0; $z < $y;$z ++)
        {
          $cd = $rd->items->[$z];
      $txtstream->WriteLine("<td             style='color:navy;font-size:10px;font-
family:Cambria, serif;' align='left' nowrap><div>"   . $cd->Items->[$a]   .
"</div></td>");
        }
      $txtstream->WriteLine("</tr>")
    }
```

Vertical Using A Link

```
    for($a=0; $a < length($nd->keys);$a ++)
    {
      $txtstream->WriteLine("<tr><th              style='color:darkred;font-
size:10px;font-family:Cambria, serif;' align='left' nowrap>"   . $nd->items->[$a] .
"</th>");
        for($z=0; $z < $y;$z ++)
        {
          $cd = $rd->items->[$z];
      $txtstream->WriteLine("<td style='font-family:Calibri, Sans-Serif;font-size:
12px;color:navy;' align='left' nowrap='true'><a href='" . $cd->Items->[$a] . "'>" .
$cd->Items->[$a] . "</a></td>\" . vbcrlf)");
        }
      $txtstream->WriteLine("</tr>");
```

```
        }
```

Vertical Using A ListBox

```
    for($a=0; $a < length($nd->keys);$a ++)
    {
        $txtstream->WriteLine("<tr><th                 style='color:darkred;font-
size:10px;font-family:Cambria, serif;' align='left' nowrap>"  . $nd->items->[$a] .
"</th>");
        for($z=0; $z < $y;$z ++)
        {
          $cd = $rd->items->[$z];
            $txtstream->WriteLine("<td        style='font-family:Calibri,      Sans-
Serif;font-size:     12px;color:navy;'      align='left'      nowrap='true'><select
multiple><option value = '"  . $cd->Items->[$a]  . "'>"  . $cd->Items->[$a]  .
"</option></select></td>\"  . vbcrlf)");
        }
        $txtstream->WriteLine("</tr>");
    }
```

Vertical Using A Span

```
    for($a=0; $a < length($nd->keys);$a ++)
    {
        $txtstream->WriteLine("<tr><th                 style='color:darkred;font-
size:10px;font-family:Cambria, serif;' align='left' nowrap>"  . $nd->items->[$a] .
"</th>");
        for($z=0; $z < $y;$z ++)
        {
          $cd = $rd->items->[$z];
        $txtstream->WriteLine("<td           style='color:navy;font-size:10px;font-
family:Cambria, serif;'  align='left'  nowrap><span>"   . $cd->Items->[$a]   .
"</span></td>");
        }
        $txtstream->WriteLine("</tr>");
    }
```

Vertical Using A Textarea

```
    for($a=0; $a < length($nd->keys);$a ++)
```

```
     {
     $txtstream->WriteLine("<tr><th                style='color:darkred;font-
size:10px;font-family:Cambria, serif;' align='left' nowrap>" . $nd->items->[$a] .
"</th>");
          for($z=0; $z < $y;$z ++)
          {
             $cd = $rd->items->[$z];
     $txtstream->WriteLine("<td              style='color:navy;font-size:10px;font-
family:Cambria, serif;' align='left' nowrap><textarea>" . $cd->Items->[$a]   .
"</textarea></td>");
          }
          $txtstream->WriteLine("</tr>");
     }
```

Vertical Using A TextBox

```
     for($a=0; $a < length($nd->keys);$a ++)
     {
     $txtstream->WriteLine("<tr><th                style='color:darkred;font-
size:10px;font-family:Cambria, serif;' align='left' nowrap>" . $nd->items->[$a] .
"</th>");
          for($z=0; $z < $y;$z ++)
          {
             $cd = $rd->items->[$z];
     $txtstream->WriteLine("<td              style='color:navy;font-size:10px;font-
family:Cambria, serif;' align='left' nowrap><input Type=text value=\"\"   . $cd-
>Items->[$a] . \"\"></input></td>");
          }
          $txtstream->WriteLine("</tr>");
     }
```

End Code

```
     $txtstream->WriteLine("</table>");
     $txtstream->WriteLine("</body>");
     $txtstream->WriteLine("</html>");
     $txtstream->Close();
     }
```

HTML TABLES

```
function Write_The_Code()
{

    $ws = Win32::OLE->new("WScript.Shell");
    $filename = $ws->CurrentDirectory . "\\Win32_Process.hta";
    $fso = Win32::OLE->new("Scripting.FileSystemObject");
    var txtstream = $fso->OpenTextFile(filename, 2, true, -2);
    $txtstream->WriteLine("<html>");
    $txtstream->WriteLine("<head>");
    $txtstream->WriteLine("<title>Win32_Process</title>");
    $txtstream->WriteLine("</head>");
    $txtstream->WriteLine("<body>");
    $txtstream->WriteLine("<table  boder=1 cellpadding=2 cellspacing=2>");
```

Horizontal No Additional Tags

```
    for($z=0; $z < $y;$z ++)
    {
        $txtstream->WriteLine("<tr>");
        $cd = $rd->items->[$z];
        for($a=0; $a < length($nd->keys);$a ++)
        {
```

```
        $txtstream->WriteLine("<td        style='color:navy;font-size:10px;font-
family:Cambria, serif;' align='left' nowrap>" . $cd->Items->[$a] . "</td>");
        }
        $txtstream->WriteLine("</tr>");
    }
```

Horizontal Using A Button

```
    for($z=0; $z < $y;$z ++)
    {
        $txtstream->WriteLine("<tr>");
        $cd = $rd->items->[$z];
        for($a=0; $a < length($nd->keys);$a ++)
        {
        $txtstream->WriteLine("<td        style='color:navy;font-size:10px;font-
family:Cambria, serif;' align='left' nowrap><input Type= button value=\"\"  . $cd-
>Items->[$a] . \"\"></input></td>");
        }
        $txtstream->WriteLine("</tr>");
    }
```

Horizontal Using A ComboBox

```
    for($z=0; $z < $y;$z ++)
    {
        $txtstream->WriteLine("<tr>");
        $cd = $rd->items->[$z];
        for($a=0; $a < length($nd->keys);$a ++)
        {
        $txtstream->WriteLine("<td        style='font-family:Calibri,    Sans-
Serif;font-size: 12px;color:navy;' align='left' nowrap='true'><select><option value =
'"  . $cd->Items->[$a] . "'>" . $cd->Items->[$a] . "</option></select></td>\"  .
vbcrlf)");
        }
        $txtstream->WriteLine("</tr>");
    }
```

Horizontal Using A Div

```
for($z=0; $z < $y;$z ++)
{
    $txtstream->WriteLine("<tr>");
    $cd = $rd->items->[$z];
    for($a=0; $a < length($nd->keys);$a ++)
    {

        $txtstream->WriteLine("<td        style='color:navy;font-size:10px;font-
family:Cambria,  serif;'  align='left'  nowrap><div>"    . $cd->Items->[$a]    .
"</div></td>");

    }
    $txtstream->WriteLine("</tr>");
}
```

Horizontal Using A Link

```
for($z=0; $z < $y;$z ++)
{
    $txtstream->WriteLine("<tr>");
    $cd = $rd->items->[$z];
    for($a=0; $a < length($nd->keys);$a ++)
    {
    $txtstream->WriteLine("<td style='font-family:Calibri, Sans-Serif;font-size:
12px;color:navy;' align='left' nowrap='true'><a href='" . $cd->Items->[$a] . "'>" .
$cd->Items->[$a] . "</a></td>\" . vbcrlf)");
    }
    $txtstream->WriteLine("</tr>");
}
```

Horizontal Using A ListBox

```
for(var d = 0;d < values.length;d ++
{
    $txtstream->WriteLine("<tr>");
```

```
    $cd = $rd->items->[$z];
    for($a=0; $a < length($nd->keys);$a ++)
    {
        $txtstream->WriteLine("<td         style='font-family:Calibri,        Sans-
Serif;font-size:    12px;color:navy;'    align='left'       nowrap='true'><select
multiple><option value = '"   . $cd->Items->[$a]   . "'>"   . $cd->Items->[$a]   .
"</option></select></td>\"  . vbcrlf)");
    }
    $txtstream->WriteLine("</tr>");
}
```

Horizontal Using A Span

```
for(var d = 0;d < values.length;d ++
{
    $txtstream->WriteLine("<tr>");
    $cd = $rd->items->[$z];
    for($a=0; $a < length($nd->keys);$a ++)
    {
        $txtstream->WriteLine("<td         style='color:navy;font-size:10px;font-
family:Cambria,  serif;'  align='left'  nowrap><span>"   .  $cd->Items->[$a]   .
"</span></td>");
    }
    $txtstream->WriteLine("</tr>");
}
```

Horizontal Using A Textarea

```
for(var d = 0;d < values.length;d ++
{
    $txtstream->WriteLine("<tr>");
    $cd = $rd->items->[$z];
    for($a=0; $a < length($nd->keys);$a ++)
    {
```

```
        $txtstream->WriteLine("<td        style='color:navy;font-size:10px;font-
family:Cambria, serif;' align='left' nowrap><textarea>"   . $cd->Items->[$a]   .
"</textarea></td>");
        }
        $txtstream->WriteLine("</tr>");
    }
```

Horizontal Using A TextBox

```
    for(var d = 0;d < values.length;d ++
    {
        $txtstream->WriteLine("<tr>");
        $cd = $rd->items->[$z];
        for($a=0; $a < length($nd->keys);$a ++)
        {
            $txtstream->WriteLine("<td        style='color:navy;font-size:10px;font-
family:Cambria, serif;' align='left' nowrap><input Type=text value=\"\"   . $cd-
>Items->[$a] . \"\"></input></td>");

        }
        $txtstream->WriteLine("</tr>");
    }
```

Vertical No Additional Controls

```
    for($a=0; $a < length($nd->keys);$a ++)
    {
        $txtstream->WriteLine("<tr><th                    style='color:darkred;font-
size:10px;font-family:Cambria, serif;' align='left' nowrap>"   . $nd->items->[$a] .
"</th>");
        for($z-0; $z < $y;$z ++)
        {
            $cd = $rd->items->[$z];
        $txtstream->WriteLine("<td        style='color:navy;font-size:10px;font-
family:Cambria, serif;' align='left' nowrap>"  . $cd->Items->[$a] . "</td>");
        }
        $txtstream->WriteLine("</tr>");
```

```
}
```

Vertical Using A Button

```
for($a=0; $a < length($nd->keys);$a ++)
{
    $txtstream->WriteLine("<tr><th                    style='color:darkred;font-
size:10px;font-family:Cambria, serif;' align='left' nowrap>"  . $nd->items->[$a] .
"</th>");
    for($z=0; $z < $y;$z ++)
    {
    $cd = $rd->items->[$z];
    $txtstream->WriteLine("<td            style='color:navy;font-size:10px;font-
family:Cambria, serif;' align='left' nowrap><input Type= button value=\"\"  . $cd-
>Items->[$a]  . \"\"></input></td>");
    }
        $txtstream->WriteLine("</tr>");
    }
```

Vertical Using A ComboBox

```
for($a=0; $a < length($nd->keys);$a ++)
{
    $txtstream->WriteLine("<tr><th                    style='color:darkred;font-
size:10px;font-family:Cambria, serif;' align='left' nowrap>"  . $nd->items->[$a] .
"</th>");
        for($z=0; $z < $y;$z ++)
        {
        $cd = $rd->items->[$z];
    $txtstream->WriteLine("<td style='font-family:Calibri, Sans-Serif;font-size:
12px;color:navy;' align='left'  nowrap='true'><select><option value = '"   . $cd-
>Items->[$a]  . "'>" . $cd->Items->[$a]  . "</option></select></td>\"  . vbcrlf)");
        }
        $txtstream->WriteLine("</tr>");
    }
```

Vertical Using A Div

```
for($a=0; $a < length($nd->keys);$a ++)
{
    $txtstream->WriteLine("<tr><th                style='color:darkred;font-
size:10px;font-family:Cambria, serif;' align='left' nowrap>" . $nd->items->[$a] .
"</th>");
        for($z=0; $z < $y;$z ++)
        {
            $cd = $rd->items->[$z];
    $txtstream->WriteLine("<td              style='color:navy;font-size:10px;font-
family:Cambria,  serif;'  align='left'  nowrap><div>"    .  $cd->Items->[$a]    .
"</div></td>");
        }
        $txtstream->WriteLine("</tr>")
}
```

Vertical Using A Link

```
for($a=0; $a < length($nd->keys);$a ++)
{
    $txtstream->WriteLine("<tr><th                style='color:darkred;font-
size:10px;font-family:Cambria, serif;' align='left' nowrap>" . $nd->items->[$a] .
"</th>");
        for($z=0; $z < $y;$z ++)
        {
            $cd = $rd->items->[$z];
    $txtstream->WriteLine("<td style='font-family:Calibri, Sans-Serif;font-size:
12px;color:navy;' align='left' nowrap='true'><a href='" . $cd->Items->[$a] . "'>" .
$cd->Items->[$a] . "</a></td>\" . vbcrlf)");
        }
        $txtstream->WriteLine("</tr>");
}
```

Vertical Using A ListBox

```
for($a=0; $a < length($nd->keys);$a ++)
{
```

```
$txtstream->WriteLine("<tr><th                style='color:darkred;font-
size:10px;font-family:Cambria, serif;' align='left' nowrap>" . $nd->items->[$a] .
"</th>");
          for($z=0; $z < $y;$z ++)
          {
            $cd = $rd->items->[$z];
            $txtstream->WriteLine("<td       style='font-family:Calibri,       Sans-
Serif;font-size:    12px;color:navy;'       align='left'      nowrap='true'><select
multiple><option value = '"  . $cd->Items->[$a]  . "'>"  . $cd->Items->[$a]  .
"</option></select></td>\" . vbcrlf)");
          }
          $txtstream->WriteLine("</tr>");
      }
```

Vertical Using A Span

```
    for($a=0; $a < length($nd->keys);$a ++)
    {
       $txtstream->WriteLine("<tr><th                style='color:darkred;font-
size:10px;font-family:Cambria, serif;' align='left' nowrap>" . $nd->items->[$a] .
"</th>");
          for($z=0; $z < $y;$z ++)
          {
            $cd = $rd->items->[$z];
       $txtstream->WriteLine("<td            style='color:navy;font-size:10px;font-
family:Cambria,  serif;'  align='left'  nowrap><span>"   . $cd->Items->[$a]   .
"</span></td>");
          }
          $txtstream->WriteLine("</tr>");
      }
```

Vertical Using A Textarea

```
    for($a=0; $a < length($nd->keys);$a ++)
    {
       $txtstream->WriteLine("<tr><th                style='color:darkred;font-
size:10px;font-family:Cambria, serif;' align='left' nowrap>" . $nd->items->[$a] .
"</th>");
          for($z=0; $z < $y;$z ++)
          {
             $cd = $rd->items->[$z];
```

```
        $txtstream->WriteLine("<td            style='color:navy;font-size:10px;font-
family:Cambria, serif;' align='left' nowrap><textarea>"  . $cd->Items->[$a]  .
"</textarea></td>");
        }
        $txtstream->WriteLine("</tr>");
    }
```

Vertical Using A TextBox

```
    for($a=0; $a < length($nd->keys);$a ++)
    {
        $txtstream->WriteLine("<tr><th            style='color:darkred;font-
size:10px;font-family:Cambria, serif;' align='left' nowrap>"  . $nd->items->[$a] .
"</th>");
        for($z=0; $z < $y;$z ++)
        {
            $cd = $rd->items->[$z];
        $txtstream->WriteLine("<td            style='color:navy;font-size:10px;font-
family:Cambria, serif;' align='left' nowrap><input Type=text value=\"\"  . $cd-
>Items->[$a] . \"\"></input></td>");
        }
        $txtstream->WriteLine("</tr>");
    }
```

End Code

```
    $txtstream->WriteLine("</table>");
    $txtstream->WriteLine("</body>");
    $txtstream->WriteLine("</html>");
    $txtstream->Close();
}
```

Stylesheets
Decorating your web pages

BELOW ARE SOME STYLESHEETS I COOKED UP THAT I LIKE AND THINK YOU MIGHT TOO. Don't worry I won't be offended if you take and modify to your hearts delight. Please do!

NONE

```
$txtstream->WriteLine('<style type='text/css'>")
$txtstream->WriteLine("    th")
$txtstream->WriteLine("    }")
$txtstream->WriteLine("    COLOR: darkred;")
$txtstream->WriteLine("    BACKGROUND-COLOR: white;")
$txtstream->WriteLine("    FONT-FAMILY:font-family: Cambria, serif;")
$txtstream->WriteLine("    FONT-SIZE: 12px;")
$txtstream->WriteLine("    text-align: left;")
$txtstream->WriteLine("    white-Space: nowrap;")
$txtstream->WriteLine("    }")
$txtstream->WriteLine("    td")
$txtstream->WriteLine("    }")
$txtstream->WriteLine("    COLOR: navy;")
```

```
$txtstream->WriteLine("   BACKGROUND-COLOR: white;")
$txtstream->WriteLine("   FONT-FAMILY: font-family: Cambria, serif;")
$txtstream->WriteLine("   FONT-SIZE: 12px;")
$txtstream->WriteLine("   text-align: left;")
$txtstream->WriteLine("   white-Space: nowrap;")
$txtstream->WriteLine("   }")
$txtstream->WriteLine("   </style>');
```

BLACK AND WHITE TEXT

```
$txtstream->WriteLine("   <style type='text/css'>');
$txtstream->WriteLine("   th")
$txtstream->WriteLine("   }")
$txtstream->WriteLine("      COLOR: white;")
$txtstream->WriteLine("      BACKGROUND-COLOR: black;")
$txtstream->WriteLine("      FONT-FAMILY:font-family: Cambria, serif;")
$txtstream->WriteLine("      FONT-SIZE: 12px;")
$txtstream->WriteLine("      text-align: left;")
$txtstream->WriteLine("      white-Space: nowrap;")
$txtstream->WriteLine("   }")
$txtstream->WriteLine("   td")
$txtstream->WriteLine("   }")
$txtstream->WriteLine("      COLOR: white;")
$txtstream->WriteLine("      BACKGROUND-COLOR: black;")
$txtstream->WriteLine("      FONT-FAMILY: font-family: Cambria, serif;")
$txtstream->WriteLine("      FONT-SIZE: 12px;")
$txtstream->WriteLine("      text-align: left;")
$txtstream->WriteLine("      white-Space: nowrap;")
$txtstream->WriteLine("   }")
$txtstream->WriteLine("   div")
$txtstream->WriteLine("   }")
$txtstream->WriteLine("      COLOR: white;")
```

```
$txtstream->WriteLine("    BACKGROUND-COLOR: black;")
$txtstream->WriteLine("    FONT-FAMILY: font-family: Cambria, serif;")
$txtstream->WriteLine("    FONT-SIZE: 10px;")
$txtstream->WriteLine("    text-align: left;")
$txtstream->WriteLine("    white-Space: nowrap;")
$txtstream->WriteLine("  }")
$txtstream->WriteLine("  span")
$txtstream->WriteLine("  }")
$txtstream->WriteLine("    COLOR: white;")
$txtstream->WriteLine("    BACKGROUND-COLOR: black;")
$txtstream->WriteLine("    FONT-FAMILY: font-family: Cambria, serif;")
$txtstream->WriteLine("    FONT-SIZE: 10px;")
$txtstream->WriteLine("    text-align: left;")
$txtstream->WriteLine("    white-Space: nowrap;")
$txtstream->WriteLine("    display:inline-block;")
$txtstream->WriteLine("    width: 100%;")
$txtstream->WriteLine("  }")
$txtstream->WriteLine("  textarea")
$txtstream->WriteLine("  }")
$txtstream->WriteLine("    COLOR: white;")
$txtstream->WriteLine("    BACKGROUND-COLOR: black;")
$txtstream->WriteLine("    FONT-FAMILY: font-family: Cambria, serif;")
$txtstream->WriteLine("    FONT-SIZE: 10px;")
$txtstream->WriteLine("    text-align: left;")
$txtstream->WriteLine("    white-Space: nowrap;")
$txtstream->WriteLine("    width: 100%;")
$txtstream->WriteLine("  }")
$txtstream->WriteLine("  select")
$txtstream->WriteLine("  }")
$txtstream->WriteLine("    COLOR: white;")
$txtstream->WriteLine("    BACKGROUND-COLOR: black;")
$txtstream->WriteLine("    FONT-FAMILY: font-family: Cambria, serif;")
$txtstream->WriteLine("    FONT-SIZE: 10px;")
```

```
$txtstream->WriteLine("      text-align: left;")
$txtstream->WriteLine("      white-Space: nowrap;")
$txtstream->WriteLine("      width: 100%;")
$txtstream->WriteLine("   }")
$txtstream->WriteLine("   input")
$txtstream->WriteLine("   }")
$txtstream->WriteLine("      COLOR: white;")
$txtstream->WriteLine("      BACKGROUND-COLOR: black;")
$txtstream->WriteLine("      FONT-FAMILY: font-family: Cambria, serif;")
$txtstream->WriteLine("      FONT-SIZE: 12px;")
$txtstream->WriteLine("      text-align: left;")
$txtstream->WriteLine("      display:table-cell;")
$txtstream->WriteLine("      white-Space: nowrap;")
$txtstream->WriteLine("   }")
$txtstream->WriteLine("   h1 }")
$txtstream->WriteLine("   color: antiquewhite;")
$txtstream->WriteLine("   text-shadow: 1px 1px 1px black;")
$txtstream->WriteLine("   padding: 3px;")
$txtstream->WriteLine("   text-align: center;")
$txtstream->WriteLine("      box-shadow: inset 2px 2px 5px rgba(0,0,0,0.5);,
inset -2px -2px 5px rgba(255,255,255,0.5);;")
$txtstream->WriteLine("   }")
$txtstream->WriteLine("   </style>');
```

COLORED TEXT

```
$txtstream->WriteLine("   <style type='text/css'>');
$txtstream->WriteLine("   th")
$txtstream->WriteLine("   }")
$txtstream->WriteLine("      COLOR: darkred;")
$txtstream->WriteLine("      BACKGROUND-COLOR: #eeeeee;")
$txtstream->WriteLine("      FONT-FAMILY:font-family: Cambria, serif;")
$txtstream->WriteLine("      FONT-SIZE: 12px;")
```

```
$txtstream->WriteLine("      text-align: left;")
$txtstream->WriteLine("      white-Space: nowrap;")
$txtstream->WriteLine("   }")
$txtstream->WriteLine("   td")
$txtstream->WriteLine("   }")
$txtstream->WriteLine("      COLOR: navy;")
$txtstream->WriteLine("      BACKGROUND-COLOR: #eeeeee;")
$txtstream->WriteLine("      FONT-FAMILY: font-family: Cambria, serif;")
$txtstream->WriteLine("      FONT-SIZE: 12px;")
$txtstream->WriteLine("      text-align: left;")
$txtstream->WriteLine("      white-Space: nowrap;")
$txtstream->WriteLine("   }")
$txtstream->WriteLine("   div")
$txtstream->WriteLine("   }")
$txtstream->WriteLine("      COLOR: white;")
$txtstream->WriteLine("      BACKGROUND-COLOR: navy;")
$txtstream->WriteLine("      FONT-FAMILY: font-family: Cambria, serif;")
$txtstream->WriteLine("      FONT-SIZE: 10px;")
$txtstream->WriteLine("      text-align: left;")
$txtstream->WriteLine("      white-Space: nowrap;")
$txtstream->WriteLine("   }")
$txtstream->WriteLine("   span")
$txtstream->WriteLine("   }")
$txtstream->WriteLine("      COLOR: white;")
$txtstream->WriteLine("      BACKGROUND-COLOR: navy;")
$txtstream->WriteLine("      FONT-FAMILY: font-family: Cambria, serif;")
$txtstream->WriteLine("      FONT-SIZE: 10px;")
$txtstream->WriteLine("      text-align: left;")
$txtstream->WriteLine("      white-Space: nowrap;")
$txtstream->WriteLine("      display:inline-block;")
$txtstream->WriteLine("      width: 100%;")
$txtstream->WriteLine("   }")
$txtstream->WriteLine("   textarea")
```

```
$txtstream->WriteLine("    }")
$txtstream->WriteLine("       COLOR: white;")
$txtstream->WriteLine("       BACKGROUND-COLOR: navy;")
$txtstream->WriteLine("       FONT-FAMILY: font-family: Cambria, serif;")
$txtstream->WriteLine("       FONT-SIZE: 10px;")
$txtstream->WriteLine("       text-align: left;")
$txtstream->WriteLine("       white-Space: nowrap;")
$txtstream->WriteLine("       width: 100%;")
$txtstream->WriteLine("    }")
$txtstream->WriteLine("    select")
$txtstream->WriteLine("    }")
$txtstream->WriteLine("       COLOR: white;")
$txtstream->WriteLine("       BACKGROUND-COLOR: navy;")
$txtstream->WriteLine("       FONT-FAMILY: font-family: Cambria, serif;")
$txtstream->WriteLine("       FONT-SIZE: 10px;")
$txtstream->WriteLine("       text-align: left;")
$txtstream->WriteLine("       white-Space: nowrap;")
$txtstream->WriteLine("       width: 100%;")
$txtstream->WriteLine("    }")
$txtstream->WriteLine("    input")
$txtstream->WriteLine("    }")
$txtstream->WriteLine("       COLOR: white;")
$txtstream->WriteLine("       BACKGROUND-COLOR: navy;")
$txtstream->WriteLine("       FONT-FAMILY: font-family: Cambria, serif;")
$txtstream->WriteLine("       FONT-SIZE: 12px;")
$txtstream->WriteLine("       text-align: left;")
$txtstream->WriteLine("       display:table-cell;")
$txtstream->WriteLine("       white-Space: nowrap;")
$txtstream->WriteLine("    }")
$txtstream->WriteLine("    h1 }")
$txtstream->WriteLine("    color: antiquewhite;")
$txtstream->WriteLine("    text-shadow: 1px 1px 1px black;")
$txtstream->WriteLine("    padding: 3px;")
```

```
$txtstream->WriteLine(" text-align: center;")
$txtstream->WriteLine("    box-shadow: inset 2px 2px 5px rgba(0,0,0,0.5);,
inset -2px -2px 5px rgba(255,255,255,0.5);;")
$txtstream->WriteLine("  }")
$txtstream->WriteLine("  </style>');
```

OSCILLATING ROW COLORS

```
$txtstream->WriteLine(" <style>');
$txtstream->WriteLine(" th")
$txtstream->WriteLine(" }")
$txtstream->WriteLine("    COLOR: white;")
$txtstream->WriteLine("    BACKGROUND-COLOR: navy;")
$txtstream->WriteLine("    FONT-FAMILY:font-family: Cambria, serif;")
$txtstream->WriteLine("    FONT-SIZE: 12px;")
$txtstream->WriteLine("    text-align: left;")
$txtstream->WriteLine("    white-Space: nowrap;")
$txtstream->WriteLine("  }")
$txtstream->WriteLine(" td")
$txtstream->WriteLine(" }")
$txtstream->WriteLine("    COLOR: navy;")
$txtstream->WriteLine("    FONT-FAMILY: font-family: Cambria, serif;")
$txtstream->WriteLine("    FONT-SIZE: 12px;")
$txtstream->WriteLine("    text-align: left;")
$txtstream->WriteLine("    white-Space: nowrap;")
$txtstream->WriteLine("  }")
$txtstream->WriteLine(" div")
$txtstream->WriteLine(" }")
$txtstream->WriteLine("    COLOR: navy;")
$txtstream->WriteLine("    FONT-FAMILY: font-family: Cambria, serif;")
$txtstream->WriteLine("    FONT-SIZE: 12px;")
```

```
$txtstream->WriteLine("    text-align: left;")
$txtstream->WriteLine("    white-Space: nowrap;")
$txtstream->WriteLine("  }")
$txtstream->WriteLine("  span")
$txtstream->WriteLine("  }")
$txtstream->WriteLine("    COLOR: navy;")
$txtstream->WriteLine("    FONT-FAMILY: font-family: Cambria, serif;")
$txtstream->WriteLine("    FONT-SIZE: 12px;")
$txtstream->WriteLine("    text-align: left;")
$txtstream->WriteLine("    white-Space: nowrap;")
$txtstream->WriteLine("    width: 100%;")
$txtstream->WriteLine("  }")
$txtstream->WriteLine("  textarea")
$txtstream->WriteLine("  }")
$txtstream->WriteLine("    COLOR: navy;")
$txtstream->WriteLine("    FONT-FAMILY: font-family: Cambria, serif;")
$txtstream->WriteLine("    FONT-SIZE: 12px;")
$txtstream->WriteLine("    text-align: left;")
$txtstream->WriteLine("    white-Space: nowrap;")
$txtstream->WriteLine("    display:inline-block;")
$txtstream->WriteLine("    width: 100%;")
$txtstream->WriteLine("  }")
$txtstream->WriteLine("  select")
$txtstream->WriteLine("  }")
$txtstream->WriteLine("    COLOR: navy;")
$txtstream->WriteLine("    FONT-FAMILY: font-family: Cambria, serif;")
$txtstream->WriteLine("    FONT-SIZE: 10px;")
$txtstream->WriteLine("    text-align: left;")
$txtstream->WriteLine("    white-Space: nowrap;")
$txtstream->WriteLine("    display:inline-block;")
$txtstream->WriteLine("    width: 100%;")
$txtstream->WriteLine("  }")
$txtstream->WriteLine("  input")
```

```
$txtstream->WriteLine("    }")
$txtstream->WriteLine("        COLOR: navy;")
$txtstream->WriteLine("        FONT-FAMILY: font-family: Cambria, serif;")
$txtstream->WriteLine("        FONT-SIZE: 12px;")
$txtstream->WriteLine("        text-align: left;")
$txtstream->WriteLine("        display:table-cell;")
$txtstream->WriteLine("        white-Space: nowrap;")
$txtstream->WriteLine("    }")
$txtstream->WriteLine("    h1 }")
$txtstream->WriteLine("    color: antiquewhite;")
$txtstream->WriteLine("    text-shadow: 1px 1px 1px black;")
$txtstream->WriteLine("    padding: 3px;")
$txtstream->WriteLine("    text-align: center;")
$txtstream->WriteLine("      box-shadow: inset 2px 2px 5px rgba(0,0,0,0.5);,
inset -2px -2px 5px rgba(255,255,255,0.5);;")
$txtstream->WriteLine("    }")
$txtstream->WriteLine("    tr:nth-child(even);}background-color:#f2f2f2;}")
$txtstream->WriteLine("           tr:nth-child(odd);}background-color:#cccccc;
color:#f2f2f2;}")
$txtstream->WriteLine("    </style>');

GHOST DECORATED

$txtstream->WriteLine("    <style type='text/css'>');
$txtstream->WriteLine("    th")
$txtstream->WriteLine("    }")
$txtstream->WriteLine("        COLOR: black;")
$txtstream->WriteLine("        BACKGROUND-COLOR: white;")
$txtstream->WriteLine("        FONT-FAMILY:font-family: Cambria, serif;")
$txtstream->WriteLine("        FONT-SIZE: 12px;")
$txtstream->WriteLine("        text-align: left;")
$txtstream->WriteLine("        white-Space: nowrap;")
$txtstream->WriteLine("    }")
```

```
$txtstream->WriteLine("    td")
$txtstream->WriteLine("    }")
$txtstream->WriteLine("      COLOR: black;")
$txtstream->WriteLine("      BACKGROUND-COLOR: white;")
$txtstream->WriteLine("      FONT-FAMILY: font-family: Cambria, serif;")
$txtstream->WriteLine("      FONT-SIZE: 12px;")
$txtstream->WriteLine("      text-align: left;")
$txtstream->WriteLine("      white-Space: nowrap;")
$txtstream->WriteLine("    }")
$txtstream->WriteLine("    div")
$txtstream->WriteLine("    }")
$txtstream->WriteLine("      COLOR: black;")
$txtstream->WriteLine("      BACKGROUND-COLOR: white;")
$txtstream->WriteLine("      FONT-FAMILY: font-family: Cambria, serif;")
$txtstream->WriteLine("      FONT-SIZE: 10px;")
$txtstream->WriteLine("      text-align: left;")
$txtstream->WriteLine("      white-Space: nowrap;")
$txtstream->WriteLine("    }")
$txtstream->WriteLine("    span")
$txtstream->WriteLine("    }")
$txtstream->WriteLine("      COLOR: black;")
$txtstream->WriteLine("      BACKGROUND-COLOR: white;")
$txtstream->WriteLine("      FONT-FAMILY: font-family: Cambria, serif;")
$txtstream->WriteLine("      FONT-SIZE: 10px;")
$txtstream->WriteLine("      text-align: left;")
$txtstream->WriteLine("      white-Space: nowrap;")
$txtstream->WriteLine("      display:inline-block;")
$txtstream->WriteLine("      width: 100%;")
$txtstream->WriteLine("    }")
$txtstream->WriteLine("    textarea")
$txtstream->WriteLine("    }")
$txtstream->WriteLine("      COLOR: black;")
$txtstream->WriteLine("      BACKGROUND-COLOR: white;")
```

```
$txtstream->WriteLine("      FONT-FAMILY: font-family: Cambria, serif;")
$txtstream->WriteLine("      FONT-SIZE: 10px;")
$txtstream->WriteLine("      text-align: left;")
$txtstream->WriteLine("      white-Space: nowrap;")
$txtstream->WriteLine("      width: 100%;")
$txtstream->WriteLine("   }")
$txtstream->WriteLine("   select")
$txtstream->WriteLine("   }")
$txtstream->WriteLine("      COLOR: black;")
$txtstream->WriteLine("      BACKGROUND-COLOR: white;")
$txtstream->WriteLine("      FONT-FAMILY: font-family: Cambria, serif;")
$txtstream->WriteLine("      FONT-SIZE: 10px;")
$txtstream->WriteLine("      text-align: left;")
$txtstream->WriteLine("      white-Space: nowrap;")
$txtstream->WriteLine("      width: 100%;")
$txtstream->WriteLine("   }")
$txtstream->WriteLine("   input")
$txtstream->WriteLine("   }")
$txtstream->WriteLine("      COLOR: black;")
$txtstream->WriteLine("      BACKGROUND-COLOR: white;")
$txtstream->WriteLine("      FONT-FAMILY: font-family: Cambria, serif;")
$txtstream->WriteLine("      FONT-SIZE: 12px;")
$txtstream->WriteLine("      text-align: left;")
$txtstream->WriteLine("      display:table-cell;")
$txtstream->WriteLine("      white-Space: nowrap;")
$txtstream->WriteLine("   }")
$txtstream->WriteLine("   h1 }")
$txtstream->WriteLine("   color: antiquewhite;")
$txtstream->WriteLine("   text-shadow: 1px 1px 1px black;")
$txtstream->WriteLine("   padding: 3px;")
$txtstream->WriteLine("   text-align: center;")
$txtstream->WriteLine("      box-shadow: inset 2px 2px 5px rgba(0,0,0,0.5);,
inset -2px -2px 5px rgba(255,255,255,0.5);;")
```

```
$txtstream->WriteLine("    }")
$txtstream->WriteLine("    </style>');

3D


$txtstream->WriteLine("    <style type='text/css'>');
$txtstream->WriteLine("    body")
$txtstream->WriteLine("    }")
$txtstream->WriteLine("       PADDING-RIGHT: 0px;")
$txtstream->WriteLine("       PADDING-LEFT: 0px;")
$txtstream->WriteLine("       PADDING-BOTTOM: 0px;")
$txtstream->WriteLine("       MARGIN: 0px;")
$txtstream->WriteLine("       COLOR: #333;")
$txtstream->WriteLine("       PADDING-TOP: 0px;")
$txtstream->WriteLine("         FONT-FAMILY: verdana, arial, helvetica, sans-
serif;")
$txtstream->WriteLine("    }")
$txtstream->WriteLine("    table")
$txtstream->WriteLine("    }")
$txtstream->WriteLine("       BORDER-RIGHT: #999999 3px solid;")
$txtstream->WriteLine("       PADDING-RIGHT: 6px;")
$txtstream->WriteLine("       PADDING-LEFT: 6px;")
$txtstream->WriteLine("       FONT-WEIGHT: Bold;")
$txtstream->WriteLine("       FONT-SIZE: 14px;")
$txtstream->WriteLine("       PADDING-BOTTOM: 6px;")
$txtstream->WriteLine("       COLOR: Peru;")
$txtstream->WriteLine("       LINE-HEIGHT: 14px;")
$txtstream->WriteLine("       PADDING-TOP: 6px;")
$txtstream->WriteLine("       BORDER-BOTTOM: #999 1px solid;")
$txtstream->WriteLine("       BACKGROUND-COLOR: #eeeeee;")
$txtstream->WriteLine("         FONT-FAMILY: verdana, arial, helvetica, sans-
serif;")
```

```
$txtstream->WriteLine("     FONT-SIZE: 12px;")
$txtstream->WriteLine("    }")
$txtstream->WriteLine("    th")
$txtstream->WriteLine("    }")
$txtstream->WriteLine("       BORDER-RIGHT: #999999 3px solid;")
$txtstream->WriteLine("       PADDING-RIGHT: 6px;")
$txtstream->WriteLine("       PADDING-LEFT: 6px;")
$txtstream->WriteLine("       FONT-WEIGHT: Bold;")
$txtstream->WriteLine("       FONT-SIZE: 14px;")
$txtstream->WriteLine("       PADDING-BOTTOM: 6px;")
$txtstream->WriteLine("       COLOR: darkred;")
$txtstream->WriteLine("       LINE-HEIGHT: 14px;")
$txtstream->WriteLine("       PADDING-TOP: 6px;")
$txtstream->WriteLine("       BORDER-BOTTOM: #999 1px solid;")
$txtstream->WriteLine("       BACKGROUND-COLOR: #eeeeee;")
$txtstream->WriteLine("       FONT-FAMILY:font-family: Cambria, serif;")
$txtstream->WriteLine("       FONT-SIZE: 12px;")
$txtstream->WriteLine("       text-align: left;")
$txtstream->WriteLine("       white-Space: nowrap;")
$txtstream->WriteLine("    }")
$txtstream->WriteLine("    .th")
$txtstream->WriteLine("    }")
$txtstream->WriteLine("       BORDER-RIGHT: #999999 2px solid;")
$txtstream->WriteLine("       PADDING-RIGHT: 6px;")
$txtstream->WriteLine("       PADDING-LEFT: 6px;")
$txtstream->WriteLine("       FONT-WEIGHT: Bold;")
$txtstream->WriteLine("       PADDING-BOTTOM: 6px;")
$txtstream->WriteLine("       COLOR: black;")
$txtstream->WriteLine("       PADDING-TOP: 6px;")
$txtstream->WriteLine("       BORDER-BOTTOM: #999 2px solid;")
$txtstream->WriteLine("       BACKGROUND-COLOR: #eeeeee;")
$txtstream->WriteLine("       FONT-FAMILY: font-family: Cambria, serif;")
$txtstream->WriteLine("       FONT-SIZE: 10px;")
```

```
$txtstream->WriteLine("      text-align: right;")
$txtstream->WriteLine("      white-Space: nowrap;")
$txtstream->WriteLine("   }")
$txtstream->WriteLine("   td")
$txtstream->WriteLine("   }")
$txtstream->WriteLine("      BORDER-RIGHT: #999999 3px solid;")
$txtstream->WriteLine("      PADDING-RIGHT: 6px;")
$txtstream->WriteLine("      PADDING-LEFT: 6px;")
$txtstream->WriteLine("      FONT-WEIGHT: Normal;")
$txtstream->WriteLine("      PADDING-BOTTOM: 6px;")
$txtstream->WriteLine("      COLOR: navy;")
$txtstream->WriteLine("      LINE-HEIGHT: 14px;")
$txtstream->WriteLine("      PADDING-TOP: 6px;")
$txtstream->WriteLine("      BORDER-BOTTOM: #999 1px solid;")
$txtstream->WriteLine("      BACKGROUND-COLOR: #eeeeee;")
$txtstream->WriteLine("      FONT-FAMILY: font-family: Cambria, serif;")
$txtstream->WriteLine("      FONT-SIZE: 12px;")
$txtstream->WriteLine("      text-align: left;")
$txtstream->WriteLine("      white-Space: nowrap;")
$txtstream->WriteLine("   }")
$txtstream->WriteLine("   div")
$txtstream->WriteLine("   }")
$txtstream->WriteLine("      BORDER-RIGHT: #999999 3px solid;")
$txtstream->WriteLine("      PADDING-RIGHT: 6px;")
$txtstream->WriteLine("      PADDING-LEFT: 6px;")
$txtstream->WriteLine("      FONT-WEIGHT: Normal;")
$txtstream->WriteLine("      PADDING-BOTTOM: 6px;")
$txtstream->WriteLine("      COLOR: white;")
$txtstream->WriteLine("      PADDING-TOP: 6px;")
$txtstream->WriteLine("      BORDER-BOTTOM: #999 1px solid;")
$txtstream->WriteLine("      BACKGROUND-COLOR: navy;")
$txtstream->WriteLine("      FONT-FAMILY: font-family: Cambria, serif;")
$txtstream->WriteLine("      FONT-SIZE: 10px;")
```

```
$txtstream->WriteLine("      text-align: left;")
$txtstream->WriteLine("      white-Space: nowrap;")
$txtstream->WriteLine("   }")
$txtstream->WriteLine("   span")
$txtstream->WriteLine("   }")
$txtstream->WriteLine("      BORDER-RIGHT: #999999 3px solid;")
$txtstream->WriteLine("      PADDING-RIGHT: 3px;")
$txtstream->WriteLine("      PADDING-LEFT: 3px;")
$txtstream->WriteLine("      FONT-WEIGHT: Normal;")
$txtstream->WriteLine("      PADDING-BOTTOM: 3px;")
$txtstream->WriteLine("      COLOR: white;")
$txtstream->WriteLine("      PADDING-TOP: 3px;")
$txtstream->WriteLine("      BORDER-BOTTOM: #999 1px solid;")
$txtstream->WriteLine("      BACKGROUND-COLOR: navy;")
$txtstream->WriteLine("      FONT-FAMILY: font-family: Cambria, serif;")
$txtstream->WriteLine("      FONT-SIZE: 10px;")
$txtstream->WriteLine("      text-align: left;")
$txtstream->WriteLine("      white-Space: nowrap;")
$txtstream->WriteLine("      display:inline-block;")
$txtstream->WriteLine("      width: 100%;")
$txtstream->WriteLine("   }")
$txtstream->WriteLine("   textarea")
$txtstream->WriteLine("   }")
$txtstream->WriteLine("      BORDER-RIGHT: #999999 3px solid;")
$txtstream->WriteLine("      PADDING-RIGHT: 3px;")
$txtstream->WriteLine("      PADDING-LEFT: 3px;")
$txtstream->WriteLine("      FONT-WEIGHT: Normal;")
$txtstream->WriteLine("      PADDING-BOTTOM: 3px;")
$txtstream->WriteLine("      COLOR: white;")
$txtstream->WriteLine("      PADDING-TOP: 3px;")
$txtstream->WriteLine("      BORDER-BOTTOM: #999 1px solid;")
$txtstream->WriteLine("      BACKGROUND-COLOR: navy;")
$txtstream->WriteLine("      FONT-FAMILY: font-family: Cambria, serif;")
```

```
$txtstream->WriteLine("    FONT-SIZE: 10px;")
$txtstream->WriteLine("    text-align: left;")
$txtstream->WriteLine("    white-Space: nowrap;")
$txtstream->WriteLine("    width: 100%;")
$txtstream->WriteLine("  }")
$txtstream->WriteLine("  select")
$txtstream->WriteLine("  }")
$txtstream->WriteLine("    BORDER-RIGHT: #999999 3px solid;")
$txtstream->WriteLine("    PADDING-RIGHT: 6px;")
$txtstream->WriteLine("    PADDING-LEFT: 6px;")
$txtstream->WriteLine("    FONT-WEIGHT: Normal;")
$txtstream->WriteLine("    PADDING-BOTTOM: 6px;")
$txtstream->WriteLine("    COLOR: white;")
$txtstream->WriteLine("    PADDING-TOP: 6px;")
$txtstream->WriteLine("    BORDER-BOTTOM: #999 1px solid;")
$txtstream->WriteLine("    BACKGROUND-COLOR: navy;")
$txtstream->WriteLine("    FONT-FAMILY: font-family: Cambria, serif;")
$txtstream->WriteLine("    FONT-SIZE: 10px;")
$txtstream->WriteLine("    text-align: left;")
$txtstream->WriteLine("    white-Space: nowrap;")
$txtstream->WriteLine("    width: 100%;")
$txtstream->WriteLine("  }")
$txtstream->WriteLine("  input")
$txtstream->WriteLine("  }")
$txtstream->WriteLine("    BORDER-RIGHT: #999999 3px solid;")
$txtstream->WriteLine("    PADDING-RIGHT: 3px;")
$txtstream->WriteLine("    PADDING-LEFT: 3px;")
$txtstream->WriteLine("    FONT-WEIGHT: Bold;")
$txtstream->WriteLine("    PADDING-BOTTOM: 3px;")
$txtstream->WriteLine("    COLOR: white;")
$txtstream->WriteLine("    PADDING-TOP: 3px;")
$txtstream->WriteLine("    BORDER-BOTTOM: #999 1px solid;")
$txtstream->WriteLine("    BACKGROUND-COLOR: navy;")
```

```
$txtstream->WriteLine("    FONT-FAMILY: font-family: Cambria, serif;")
$txtstream->WriteLine("    FONT-SIZE: 12px;")
$txtstream->WriteLine("    text-align: left;")
$txtstream->WriteLine("    display:table-cell;")
$txtstream->WriteLine("    white-Space: nowrap;")
$txtstream->WriteLine("    width: 100%;")
$txtstream->WriteLine("  }")
$txtstream->WriteLine("  h1 }")
$txtstream->WriteLine("  color: antiquewhite;")
$txtstream->WriteLine("  text-shadow: 1px 1px 1px black;")
$txtstream->WriteLine("  padding: 3px;")
$txtstream->WriteLine("  text-align: center;")
$txtstream->WriteLine("    box-shadow: inset 2px 2px 5px rgba(0,0,0,0.5);,
inset -2px -2px 5px rgba(255,255,255,0.5);;")
$txtstream->WriteLine("  }")
$txtstream->WriteLine("  </style>');
```

SHADOW BOX

```
$txtstream->WriteLine("  <style type='text/css'>');
$txtstream->WriteLine("  body")
$txtstream->WriteLine("  }")
$txtstream->WriteLine("    PADDING-RIGHT: 0px;")
$txtstream->WriteLine("    PADDING-LEFT: 0px;")
$txtstream->WriteLine("    PADDING-BOTTOM: 0px;")
$txtstream->WriteLine("    MARGIN: 0px;")
$txtstream->WriteLine("    COLOR: #333;")
$txtstream->WriteLine("    PADDING-TOP: 0px;")
$txtstream->WriteLine("      FONT-FAMILY: verdana, arial, helvetica, sans-
serif;")
$txtstream->WriteLine("  }")
$txtstream->WriteLine("  table")
$txtstream->WriteLine("  }")
```

```
$txtstream->WriteLine("        BORDER-RIGHT: #999999 1px solid;")
$txtstream->WriteLine("        PADDING-RIGHT: 1px;")
$txtstream->WriteLine("        PADDING-LEFT: 1px;")
$txtstream->WriteLine("        PADDING-BOTTOM: 1px;")
$txtstream->WriteLine("        LINE-HEIGHT: 8px;")
$txtstream->WriteLine("        PADDING-TOP: 1px;")
$txtstream->WriteLine("        BORDER-BOTTOM: #999 1px solid;")
$txtstream->WriteLine("        BACKGROUND-COLOR: #eeeeee;")
$txtstream->WriteLine("
filter:progid:DXImageTransform.Microsoft.Shadow(color='silver',        Direction=135,
Strength=16")
$txtstream->WriteLine("    }")
$txtstream->WriteLine("    th")
$txtstream->WriteLine("    }")
$txtstream->WriteLine("        BORDER-RIGHT: #999999 3px solid;")
$txtstream->WriteLine("        PADDING-RIGHT: 6px;")
$txtstream->WriteLine("        PADDING-LEFT: 6px;")
$txtstream->WriteLine("        FONT-WEIGHT: Bold;")
$txtstream->WriteLine("        FONT-SIZE: 14px;")
$txtstream->WriteLine("        PADDING-BOTTOM: 6px;")
$txtstream->WriteLine("        COLOR: darkred;")
$txtstream->WriteLine("        LINE-HEIGHT: 14px;")
$txtstream->WriteLine("        PADDING-TOP: 6px;")
$txtstream->WriteLine("        BORDER-BOTTOM: #999 1px solid;")
$txtstream->WriteLine("        BACKGROUND-COLOR: #eeeeee;")
$txtstream->WriteLine("        FONT-FAMILY: font-family: Cambria, serif;")
$txtstream->WriteLine("        FONT-SIZE: 12px;")
$txtstream->WriteLine("        text-align: left;")
$txtstream->WriteLine("        white-Space: nowrap;")
$txtstream->WriteLine("    }")
$txtstream->WriteLine("    .th")
$txtstream->WriteLine("    }")
$txtstream->WriteLine("        BORDER-RIGHT: #999999 2px solid;")
```

```
$txtstream->WriteLine("     PADDING-RIGHT: 6px;")
$txtstream->WriteLine("     PADDING-LEFT: 6px;")
$txtstream->WriteLine("     FONT-WEIGHT: Bold;")
$txtstream->WriteLine("     PADDING-BOTTOM: 6px;")
$txtstream->WriteLine("     COLOR: black;")
$txtstream->WriteLine("     PADDING-TOP: 6px;")
$txtstream->WriteLine("     BORDER-BOTTOM: #999 2px solid;")
$txtstream->WriteLine("     BACKGROUND-COLOR: #eeeeee;")
$txtstream->WriteLine("     FONT-FAMILY: font-family: Cambria, serif;")
$txtstream->WriteLine("     FONT-SIZE: 10px;")
$txtstream->WriteLine("     text-align: right;")
$txtstream->WriteLine("     white-Space: nowrap;")
$txtstream->WriteLine("   }")
$txtstream->WriteLine("   td")
$txtstream->WriteLine("   }")
$txtstream->WriteLine("     BORDER-RIGHT: #999999 3px solid;")
$txtstream->WriteLine("     PADDING-RIGHT: 6px;")
$txtstream->WriteLine("     PADDING-LEFT: 6px;")
$txtstream->WriteLine("     FONT-WEIGHT: Normal;")
$txtstream->WriteLine("     PADDING-BOTTOM: 6px;")
$txtstream->WriteLine("     COLOR: navy;")
$txtstream->WriteLine("     LINE-HEIGHT: 14px;")
$txtstream->WriteLine("     PADDING-TOP: 6px;")
$txtstream->WriteLine("     BORDER-BOTTOM: #999 1px solid;")
$txtstream->WriteLine("     BACKGROUND-COLOR: #eeeeee;")
$txtstream->WriteLine("     FONT-FAMILY: font-family: Cambria, serif;")
$txtstream->WriteLine("     FONT-SIZE: 12px;")
$txtstream->WriteLine("     text-align: left;")
$txtstream->WriteLine("     white-Space: nowrap;")
$txtstream->WriteLine("   }")
$txtstream->WriteLine("   div")
$txtstream->WriteLine("   }")
$txtstream->WriteLine("     BORDER-RIGHT: #999999 3px solid;")
```

```
$txtstream->WriteLine("      PADDING-RIGHT: 6px;")
$txtstream->WriteLine("      PADDING-LEFT: 6px;")
$txtstream->WriteLine("      FONT-WEIGHT: Normal;")
$txtstream->WriteLine("      PADDING-BOTTOM: 6px;")
$txtstream->WriteLine("      COLOR: white;")
$txtstream->WriteLine("      PADDING-TOP: 6px;")
$txtstream->WriteLine("      BORDER-BOTTOM: #999 1px solid;")
$txtstream->WriteLine("      BACKGROUND-COLOR: navy;")
$txtstream->WriteLine("      FONT-FAMILY: font-family: Cambria, serif;")
$txtstream->WriteLine("      FONT-SIZE: 10px;")
$txtstream->WriteLine("      text-align: left;")
$txtstream->WriteLine("      white-Space: nowrap;")
$txtstream->WriteLine("   }")
$txtstream->WriteLine("   span")
$txtstream->WriteLine("   }")
$txtstream->WriteLine("      BORDER-RIGHT: #999999 3px solid;")
$txtstream->WriteLine("      PADDING-RIGHT: 3px;")
$txtstream->WriteLine("      PADDING-LEFT: 3px;")
$txtstream->WriteLine("      FONT-WEIGHT: Normal;")
$txtstream->WriteLine("      PADDING-BOTTOM: 3px;")
$txtstream->WriteLine("      COLOR: white;")
$txtstream->WriteLine("      PADDING-TOP: 3px;")
$txtstream->WriteLine("      BORDER-BOTTOM: #999 1px solid;")
$txtstream->WriteLine("      BACKGROUND-COLOR: navy;")
$txtstream->WriteLine("      FONT-FAMILY: font-family: Cambria, serif;")
$txtstream->WriteLine("      FONT-SIZE: 10px;")
$txtstream->WriteLine("      text-align: left;")
$txtstream->WriteLine("      white-Space: nowrap;")
$txtstream->WriteLine("      display: inline-block;")
$txtstream->WriteLine("      width: 100%;")
$txtstream->WriteLine("   }")
$txtstream->WriteLine("   textarea")
$txtstream->WriteLine("   }")
```

```
$txtstream->WriteLine("     BORDER-RIGHT: #999999 3px solid;")
$txtstream->WriteLine("     PADDING-RIGHT: 3px;")
$txtstream->WriteLine("     PADDING-LEFT: 3px;")
$txtstream->WriteLine("     FONT-WEIGHT: Normal;")
$txtstream->WriteLine("     PADDING-BOTTOM: 3px;")
$txtstream->WriteLine("     COLOR: white;")
$txtstream->WriteLine("     PADDING-TOP: 3px;")
$txtstream->WriteLine("     BORDER-BOTTOM: #999 1px solid;")
$txtstream->WriteLine("     BACKGROUND-COLOR: navy;")
$txtstream->WriteLine("     FONT-FAMILY: font-family: Cambria, serif;")
$txtstream->WriteLine("     FONT-SIZE: 10px;")
$txtstream->WriteLine("     text-align: left;")
$txtstream->WriteLine("     white-Space: nowrap;")
$txtstream->WriteLine("     width: 100%;")
$txtstream->WriteLine("   }")
$txtstream->WriteLine("   select")
$txtstream->WriteLine("   }")
$txtstream->WriteLine("     BORDER-RIGHT: #999999 3px solid;")
$txtstream->WriteLine("     PADDING-RIGHT: 6px;")
$txtstream->WriteLine("     PADDING-LEFT: 6px;")
$txtstream->WriteLine("     FONT-WEIGHT: Normal;")
$txtstream->WriteLine("     PADDING-BOTTOM: 6px;")
$txtstream->WriteLine("     COLOR: white;")
$txtstream->WriteLine("     PADDING-TOP: 6px;")
$txtstream->WriteLine("     BORDER-BOTTOM: #999 1px solid;")
$txtstream->WriteLine("     BACKGROUND-COLOR: navy;")
$txtstream->WriteLine("     FONT-FAMILY: font-family: Cambria, serif;")
$txtstream->WriteLine("     FONT-SIZE: 10px;")
$txtstream->WriteLine("     text-align: left;")
$txtstream->WriteLine("     white-Space: nowrap;")
$txtstream->WriteLine("     width: 100%;")
$txtstream->WriteLine("   }")
$txtstream->WriteLine("   input")
```

```
$txtstream->WriteLine("    }")
$txtstream->WriteLine("        BORDER-RIGHT: #999999 3px solid;")
$txtstream->WriteLine("        PADDING-RIGHT: 3px;")
$txtstream->WriteLine("        PADDING-LEFT: 3px;")
$txtstream->WriteLine("        FONT-WEIGHT: Bold;")
$txtstream->WriteLine("        PADDING-BOTTOM: 3px;")
$txtstream->WriteLine("        COLOR: white;")
$txtstream->WriteLine("        PADDING-TOP: 3px;")
$txtstream->WriteLine("        BORDER-BOTTOM: #999 1px solid;")
$txtstream->WriteLine("        BACKGROUND-COLOR: navy;")
$txtstream->WriteLine("        FONT-FAMILY: font-family: Cambria, serif;")
$txtstream->WriteLine("        FONT-SIZE: 12px;")
$txtstream->WriteLine("        text-align: left;")
$txtstream->WriteLine("        display: table-cell;")
$txtstream->WriteLine("        white-Space: nowrap;")
$txtstream->WriteLine("        width: 100%;")
$txtstream->WriteLine("    }")
$txtstream->WriteLine("    h1 }")
$txtstream->WriteLine("    color: antiquewhite;")
$txtstream->WriteLine("    text-shadow: 1px 1px 1px black;")
$txtstream->WriteLine("    padding: 3px;")
$txtstream->WriteLine("    text-align: center;")
$txtstream->WriteLine("        box-shadow: inset 2px 2px 5px rgba(0,0,0,0.5);,
inset -2px -2px 5px rgba(255,255,255,0.5);;")
$txtstream->WriteLine("    }")
$txtstream->WriteLine("    </style>');
```

www.ingramcontent.com/pod-product-compliance
Lightning Source LLC
Chambersburg PA
CBHW070841070326
40690CB00009B/1638